JESUS & JUSTICE

Original publication 2009. Edited 2015.

Author's note: Capitalization of certain words are for emphasis only.

Printed in the United States of America

Published by
Word At Work Ministries, Inc.
P.O. Box 366 • Placentia, California 92871 • U.S.A.

www.wordatwork.org

ISBN 978-0-940252-82-0

JESUS & JUSTICE

AL HOUGHTON

Table of Contents

Foreword

Jesus came as a Suffering Servant and Savior in the gospels but in Revelation, He is the Judge of all the earth. As the Judge of all the earth, He makes believers Kingly-Priests and invites our participation. We are responsible for representing the Judge as a spiritual King. The church has done a good job witnessing for Jesus the Savior as Priests but a witness for Jesus the Judge is nearly nonexistent. Every mature believer is an agent of the heavenly court and is charged with bringing God's justice to their sphere of life. Justice was the biblical assignment for the office of King. Knowing Jesus the Judge is foundational. Learning to function as an officer of the court is a critical and necessary component for the end-time harvest.

The Judge of all the earth is recruiting agents who will boldly declare justice just as the early church did. They marched fearlessly into the jaws of their ungodly culture, declaring the Word of the Lord. Only the judgments of God can arrest the level of perversion that is attacking and assaulting the Twin Towers of culture and country. The enemy knows just what weapon to use to cause a catastrophic structural failure. America's iron core is in the fiery furnace of a cultural war. Whether it stands or falls depends on our ability to access divine justice as spiritual Kings. Tradition and seeker-sensitive Christianity have disabled the church from effectively turning the tide! At the turn of the Twentieth

Century, America had preachers who understood their spiritual authority as a King and prayed justice on their antichrist adversaries. They represented Jesus the Judge in such a strong way as to make church leaders today look like politicians masquerading as ministers.

In September of 1901, Mordecai F. Ham Jr. preached from the pulpit his grandfather had occupied for forty years and the Holy Spirit moved. He entered the ministry that day and became a fearless representative of both Jesus the Savior and Jesus the Judge. On page 32 of Edward E. Ham's biography, *50 Years on the Battle Front with Christ,* we find this account illustrating Ham's courage and convictions:

> *"On that second night it seemed all 'hell' broke loose as the moonshine crowd stole up around the church, after we had begun the meeting, and threw rocks at us. They unharnessed the horses, cut the saddle straps and stole everything they could carry off." Ham went out and confronted the ringleader, who proceeded to pull a knife on him. "Put up that knife, you coward. If you were not a coward you wouldn't pull a knife on an unarmed man. Now I'm going to ask the Lord either to convert you and your crowd or to kill you." "Do as you damn please," he snarled at me as he stalked off. I prayed, and that bully was dying the next morning. They called for me to go and pray for him, but he died before I got to his bedside. On that same day a neighborhood sawmill blew up and killed three others of the crowd. That night I announced from the pulpit that I wanted everything that had been stolen the preceding evening brought to the church on the next night and that the Lord might kill any person who tried to keep something that didn't belong to him. Twenty-four hours later I took inventory and announced that we would pray because one saddle was still missing. Some fellow in the congregation jumped up and hollered, "You needn't*

pray; it will be here in a few minutes." And it was.[1]

This is the man who won Billy Graham to the Lord.

For every Christian who grieves over the direction of their nation but is not sure what to do to change it, an answer emerges from these pages. The only difference between us and Mordecai Ham is that he discovered his calling as a King and stepped into it! Jesus is recruiting agents of justice – you are about to be drafted! The goal of this book is to recover the full measure of biblical justice that Jesus made available for every King-Priest. Our generation faces a greater dimension of the antichrist spirit than Ham's, therefore we need to see a doubling of the anointing to remove the opposition! If you have a desire to equip yourself to access the Throne for justice as Ham did, then this book is offered as the second in a series of books aimed at establishing a foundation for representing Jesus the Judge as a spiritual King. The foundation upon which this book builds is *The Sure Mercies of David.* May the promise of Isaiah 60:1-3 be yours as you study, *"Arise, shine; For your light has come! And the glory of the LORD is risen upon you. For behold, the darkness shall cover the earth, And deep darkness the people; But the LORD will arise over you, And His glory will be seen upon you. The Gentiles shall come to your light, And kings to the brightness of your rising."*

When I went to war as a Navy pilot in Vietnam it took 24 months of intensive training before I was ready to fly my first combat mission. There is a war raging over silencing the church and we may not have 24 months to prepare before significant battles are won or lost. Join God's army and locate the armory! This book is for warriors who desire to find God's armory and deliver divine ordnance.

---

1. Ham, Edward E. *50 Years on the Battle Front with Christ: A Biography of Mordecai F. Ham,* Old Kentucky Home Revivalist, 1950. 32.

Chapter 1

Foundation for Justice

In Matthew 24, when Jesus was asked about His return He gave a very detailed answer which presents us with a unique enigma. He started out saying in verses 4 and 5 that many imposters will appear and goes on to describe a dangerous sorrowful time as war and rumors of war rule where *"...nation will rise against nation and kingdom against kingdom."*

In WWII, Korea, and Viet Nam, when nation rose against nation, we knew where the enemy was. With the worldwide emergence of radical Islam, national borders have been rendered meaningless. We have transitioned to *"kingdom against kingdom"* and that means terrorists' cells can exist right next door. Every Founding Father would turn over in his grave realizing freedom of religion has slowly transformed into freedom that protects radicals whose 'religion' demands that Christians and Jews be slaughtered! To our forefathers, freedom of religion was freedom to worship – not freedom to oppress or kill! Subverting the Constitution by accepting sharia law anywhere in America would have sent previous generations to war. The magnitude of this betrayal is beyond the comprehension of previous generations but now looms as a possibility.

Jesus went on to say that offense, betrayal, and animosity would rule, then many false prophets would rise, deception would grow dramatically, and lawlessness would be everywhere. Verses 12-14 present an enigma because when lawlessness abounds the chief issue becomes injustice at every level. But even in such injustice the victorious declaration in verse 14 rings out in stark contrast to the previous descriptions. It says, *"And this gospel of the kingdom will be preached in all the world as a witness to all the nations, and then the end will come."* The picture presented is a very hostile environment in which a variety of different groups would like to kill the messengers but the messengers cannot be stopped! The message of the returning Christ will be preached in spite of all resistance. This passage imparts an absolute air of victory in verse 14, which is staunchly different from the descriptions of what transpires preceding it. In the midst of great injustice, agents of Christ arise with an immutable voice. The anointing that enabled Jesus to walk through a crowd trying to kill Him will be theirs. Are we ready to follow pioneers like Mordecai Ham and possess the fullness of Christ?

In Revelation 22:11 we are told, *"He who is unjust, let him be unjust still; he who is filthy, let him be filthy still; he who is righteous, let him be righteous still; he who is holy, let him be holy still."* The Greek word translated *"unjust"* is **ad-ee-keh-o** and it is used 'to hurt, to damage, to harm, or to be consistently criminal.' Unjust is a good description because it describes a panorama of activity which nearly takes all justice from the earth. The Greek word translated *"filthy"* is **rhoo-par-os** and it means 'to be consistently morally impure, soiled, or stained permanently.' The Greek word *"righteous"* is **dik-ah-yos-oo-nay** and it means 'virtuous, to keep the divine law, conform to God's will, embrace the biblical standard.' *"Holy"* is the Greek word **hag-ee-ad-zo** meaning 'to separate from defilement by embracing moral purity and to represent the God of righteousness.' *"Still"* means 'the crystallization and development of character until one perfectly reflects the God/god he has chosen to serve.'

Those who refuse Christ will increasingly reflect the demons they serve. Those who accept Jesus will reflect Him as Savior and Judge. Revelation specifically reaffirms what we find Jesus speaking in Matthew 24. Justice will increasingly disappear from the earth so that the only source for it comes out of God's Throne through our relationship and ability to bring His Hand upon any given situation. The days are approaching when the only justice available is what the church can bring through prayer and prophetic proclamation. A church that cannot move God's Hand in justice is a church that cannot stand to preach the gospel as a witness against all the nations.

There are issues that transcend eschatology. Some have a dispensational view of the end-times and believe the rapture is imminent. Others believe it does not happen until the end of the tribulation. And others believe Revelation has been completed. But regardless, **justice** is the end-time issue. The witness for the gospel must include both salvation and justice. Priests minister salvation. Kings minister justice. Matthew chapters 24 and 25, make very clear the price the church has to pay to witness in the midst of great persecution. The end-time church must stand and give a witness for the Lord in the midst of an ever-growing ungodly culture where justice is not available except through relationship with God and by manifestation of the Holy Spirit. Any prudent believer should be doing everything possible to prepare for this season by learning about God's justice and how to bring that justice into manifestation in any given situation. A leadership generation which refuses to train its sons and daughters in how to birth and manifest the justice of God is offering them up to destruction by refusing to prepare them for what they will need to finish their race. The Jesus of Revelation judges and makes war. Unless we partner with Him in judging and making war, we are actually working against Him by enabling the enemy to continue destroying through ungodly vessels who like Herod need to be "cut off"!

Jesus bought and paid for justice. He made justice accessible and to not pursue it with all our heart and mind would be spiritually immature. Mordecai Ham understood covenant justice. How did we lose it? The God of justice wants to demonstrate who He is in the earth long before Jesus returns physically. We have missed a major key to the Jewish harvest! Demonstrating the Kingly justice of the Messiah instead of solely preaching the Priestly compassion of the Savior will reveal to Israel the Messiah they have been seeking! When the Jews see the Jesus of justice I believe they will catapult into the Kingdom. They have been looking for Him for several thousand years. It is time we prepared a generation for the ultimate harvest and introduce them to both Jesus the Savior and Jesus the Judge. The Jesus of Mordecai Ham needs to be seen in America. Until we raise a generation to represent Jesus the Judge we have not fulfilled our mission! Jesus made us Kings and through tradition we forfeited the authority of the crown!

The power of the cross undergirds the end-time promise that enables the church to access justice covenantally. The cross has a right half and a left half, each supporting an arm of Christ signifying both the Priestly and Kingly ministries. Jesus bought and paid for justice as outlined in Colossians 1:19-23:

> *For it pleased the Father that in Him all the fullness should dwell, and by Him to reconcile all things to Himself, by Him, whether things on earth or things in heaven, having made peace through the blood of His cross. And you, who once were alienated and enemies in your mind by wicked works, yet now He has reconciled in the body of His flesh through death, to present you holy, and blameless, and irreproachable in His sight – if indeed you continue in the faith, grounded and steadfast, and are not moved away from the hope of the gospel which you heard,*

which was preached to every creature under heaven, of which I, Paul, became a minister.

Preparing to be an agent of God's justice demands that we fully accept the sacrifice of Christ for us in every dimension and in our conscience we must stand before Him *"...blameless and irreproachable."* That has to be more than a head-knowledge. It has to be a heart-reality. When the left half of the cross becomes a heart-reality then the church can enter into the resurrected, ascended, judicial, victorious right Hand of the cross as described in Colossians 2:8-10.

Colossians 2:8-10 says, *"Beware lest anyone cheat you through philosophy and empty deceit, according to the tradition of men, according to the basic principles of the world, and not according to Christ. For in Him dwells all the fullness of the Godhead bodily; and you are complete in Him, who is the head of all principality and power."* Philosophy, tradition and principles of the world all unite to steal a revelation of righteousness from every believer. Only a revelation of God's Word empowers and enables us to access divine justice. Verse 9 has ready acceptance in practically any school of theology but the application is hard to accept. Real believers all agree that in Jesus *"...dwells all the fullness of the Godhead bodily."* But verse 10 is based on the reality of verse 9. If we, in fact, believe that Jesus represented the *"...fullness of the Godhead bodily..."*.

then we are stuck with the fact that we are full in Him. In the Greek, verse 9 says, *"For in Him dwells all the* ***play-ro-ma*** *of the Godhead."* And verse 10 says, *"...and we are* ***play-ro-o*** *in Him, who is the head of all principality and power."* We are the verb, the agents of action doing what needs to be done to demonstrate fullness.

It is only when the left half of the cross becomes reality that the church can step up into the right half of authority and actually do what scripture promises such as Ephesians 3:10-12 which says, *"...to the intent that now the manifold wisdom of God might be made known by the church to the principalities and powers in the heavenly places, according to the eternal purpose which He accomplished in Christ Jesus our Lord, in whom we have boldness and access with confidence through faith in Him."* God's purpose for every believer is that through our relationship with Him we will demonstrate, teach, or instruct and make manifest the fact that principalities and powers no longer rule – God does! The tool of that judicial conflict is judgment! There is no greater way for this conflict of good and evil to play out than the justice of God being manifested through the church.

Mordecai Ham understood this a century ago:

> *...at other times he faced down stubborn oppressors of the gospel, declaring he would pray to God to either convert them or kill them. The evangelist recalls with great reluctance that deaths took place during many of his great campaigns. Ambulances would have to come and carry bodies away from our services... Many persons that openly fought a Ham meeting met with some form of violent death soon after.*[2]

It is time we realize that God has a purpose for the end-time church and that purpose demands we become agents of justice, deputized, authorized and anointed to bring justice into every place we walk. The great commission should empower us just as Joshua was told that every place his foot would tread, God had given it to him. The book of Ephesians outlines for the New Testament church that every place our foot treads we can bring the justice of God, and it is time to train a

---

2. Ham, 102-3. See also Smithers, David. "Mordecai Ham." Awake & Go! Global Prayer Network.

generation in that reality and ultimate purpose. There will rise a church without spot, wrinkle, or blemish, a victorious church who fully represents the Lord Jesus dispensing both life and death, according to what the culture requires. Joel 2:23 says the Lord gave the *"...former rain moderately..."* but the Hebrew word means 'according to what the ground requires.' Many of the enemies of the cross today threaten Kingdom purposes to the point that they are worthy of the full measure of God's justice. When led by the Spirit, proclaiming and decreeing it is an honor for every believer, *"...this honor have all his saints"* (Psalm 149:9). In today's culture, Mordecai Ham would be very busy!

An assignment for saints,
Pure, noble and just,
The ones fully sold out,
Whom God knows and trusts.

Jayne Houghton

Chapter 2

The Power of Salvation

Asking God for justice is not seeking revenge. The two are separated by a mountain of motivation and the sovereign nature of God in response to an individual's refusal to repent. There is a fail-safe filter for all judicial prayers. There is no record of man persuading God to do something that He was not willing to do. George Fox, a dissenting maverick preacher, lived from 1624 to 1691 and became the father of the Quaker Movement renowned for "turn-the-other-cheek" Christianity. Fox endured unspeakable persecution but was careful to never seek revenge. Seeking justice is entirely different as his comments on page 178-179 of his autobiography prove, where he says:

> Indeed, I could not but take notice how the **hand of the Lord** turned against the persecutors who had been the cause of my imprisonment, or had been abusive or cruel to me in it. The officer that fetched me to Holker-Hall wasted his estate, and soon after fled into Ireland. Most of the justices that were upon the bench at the sessions when I was sent to prison, died in a while after; as old Thomas Preston, Rawlinson, Porter, and Matthew West, of Borwick. Justice Fleming's wife died, and left him thirteen or fourteen motherless children. Colonel Kirby never prospered after. The chief constable, Richard Dodgson, died

> soon after, and Mount, the petty constable, and the wife of the other petty constable, John Ashburnham, who railed at me in her house, died soon after. William Knipe, the witness they brought against me, died soon after also. Hunter, the jailer of Lancaster, who was very wicked to me while I was his prisoner, was cut off in his young days; and the under-sheriff that carried me from Lancaster Prison towards Scarborough, lived not long after. And Joblin, the jailer of Durham, who was prisoner with me in Scarborough Castle, and had often incensed the Governor and soldiers against me, though he got out of prison, yet the Lord cut him off in his wickedness soon after. When I came into that country again, most of those that dwelt in Lancashire were dead, and others ruined in their estates; so that, though I did not seek revenge upon them for their actions against me contrary to the law, yet the Lord had executed His judgments upon many of them.[3]

Jesus executed justice in the 1600s – has He ever stopped? The book of Revelation demands that we prepare to be "*agents of justice*" in the last days. The Lord has been executing justice for generations. We should be asking for it! Preparing to dispense justice demands a solid foundation in our hearts and lives. Romans 1:16-17 says, *"For I am not ashamed of the gospel of Christ, for it is the power of God to salvation for everyone who believes, for the Jew first and also for the Greek. For in it the righteousness of God is revealed from faith to faith; as it is written, 'The just shall live by faith.'"* This passage reveals that salvation has three primary elements when it comes to obtaining the full measure of covenant promises. The gospel that the early church preached was centered in the resurrection of Christ who had been crucified to death, then seen and touched in resurrection. They witnessed the God Who

---

3. Jones, M.A. Litt. D., et al., eds. *George Fox An Autobiography.* 178-9.

conquered death. The first element was resurrection. By believing the report of the resurrection, righteousness was imparted. Accepting the second meant sin was washed away – remitted, obliterated, gone forever. A righteousness-consciousness must replace a sin-consciousness. Once this reality settled in, a third element emerged.

Faith toward God arose for unceasing access to the Throne. All these components woven together make the rope that opens the door to the full measure of salvation. Tradition has limited salvation to mercy for the individual violators. Salvation also includes justice for believers against those seeking their harm. A church incapable of aligning with divine justice is a church that has a lot of growing up to do. We must prepare a generation who can by faith at least duplicate the acts of the early church because the prophets promised we would double them. The perfect example of tugging this rope comes in Acts 3 where Peter at the gate of the Temple called Beautiful meets a man who is asking alms because he is a paralytic and cannot walk. Peter says to him, *"'Silver and gold I do not have, but what I do have I give you: In the name of Jesus Christ of Nazareth, rise up and walk.'"* Verses 7 and 8 state, *"And he took him by the right hand and lifted him up, and immediately his feet and ankle bones received strength. So he, leaping up, stood and walked and entered the temple with them – walking, leaping, and praising God."* This manifestation of faith imparted by Peter received by the lame man created no small stir to the point that Peter and his friends were jailed by the leaders of the Sanhedrin and examined the following day. Peter has this to say further explaining the cords woven together that make up the salvation rope.

In Acts 4:10-12 he says: *"Let it be known to you all, and to all the people of Israel, that by the name of Jesus Christ of Nazareth, whom you crucified, whom God raised from the dead, by Him this man stands here before you whole. This is the 'stone which was rejected by you builders, which has become the chief cornerstone.' Nor is there salvation in any other, for there is no other name under heaven given among men by which we must be saved."*

Personal salvation is the fruit of believing that Jesus is the Son of God, believing the historical account that He came, born of a virgin as the sinless sacrifice, died for mankind, and was resurrected on the third day. We have not only the eye witnesses of those who were present and have written their accounts but we also have the personal fruit of believing that today. Personal salvation can readily and easily be received. If we confess with our mouth and believe with our heart that Jesus is Lord, we shall be saved. Personal salvation is the fruit of believing, confessing, and receiving. The Bible-believing church agrees that salvation comes this way. We understand mercy for personal salvation. Mercy for corporate salvation is often very different. The problem for us is in making the shift in application from personal to corporate. Personal individual salvation can independently and easily be received by anyone who chooses to believe. Mercy is available for all.

Corporate salvation often has an entirely different manifestation and one that causes many New Testament believers to pause in hesitation because the path demands an understanding of justice as we embrace two very different applications of mercy. The entire church is so Priestly that extending personal mercy for an individual's sin is almost an automatic response. Having received personal mercy we readily extend it. Receiving corporate mercy is an entirely different matter. Mercy for an individual and mercy for the American nation have two very different manifestations.

The gospel is just as much the power of God to corporate salvation as it is the power of God to personal salvation. The difference is we are very comfortable ministering personal salvation as a Priest and we are very uncomfortable with invoking the covenant that brings the judgment required for corporate salvation as a King.

A great example of covenantal corporate salvation comes in Isaiah 37. Sennacherib, king of Assyria, sent his army to progressively subjugate nation after nation. No one was able to stop the Assyrian army until they stood at the gates of Jerusalem. Their leading officer wrote a letter demanding surrender. Hezekiah knew that the Jewish nation of believers had a covenant with God that offered them salvation unto protection and preservation. Upon ascending the throne Hezekiah's first act was cleansing the temple and restoring a pure altar. That timely choice established a platform to save the nation. Believers in any nation can embrace their covenant with God and can ask for corporate salvation. Isaiah 37:14-20 relates Hezekiah's prayer for corporate salvation:

> *And Hezekiah received the letter from the hand of the messengers, and read it; and Hezekiah went up to the house of the Lord, and spread it before the LORD. Then Hezekiah prayed to the LORD, saying: "O Lord of hosts, God of Israel, the One who dwells between the cherubim, You are God, You alone, of all the kingdoms of the earth. You have made heaven and earth. Incline Your ear, O LORD, and hear; open Your eyes, O LORD, and see; and hear all the words of Sennacherib, who has sent to reproach the living God. Truly, LORD, the kings of Assyria have laid waste all the nations and their lands, and have cast their gods into the fire; for they were not gods, but the work of men's hands – wood and stone. Therefore they have destroyed them. Now therefore, O LORD our God, save us from his hand, that all the kingdoms of the earth may know that You are the LORD, You alone."*

God did, but what have we learned from the heavenly response? Hezekiah prayed that all would know by what God did! This biblical pattern is one we should be repeating!

Interestingly enough right after Hezekiah released his faith in intercession asking God to honor the covenant and bring corporate salvation, Isaiah appeared with a word in answer to Hezekiah's prayer. Isaiah's word (verses 21b-22, 33-35) was:

> *Thus says the Lord God of Israel, '**Because you have prayed to Me against** Sennacherib king of Assyria, this is the word which the Lord has spoken concerning him: "The virgin, the daughter of Zion, Has despised you, laughed you to scorn; The daughter of Jerusalem has shaken her head behind your back! Therefore thus says the LORD concerning the king of Assyria: 'He shall not come into this city, Nor shoot an arrow there, Nor come before it with shield, Nor build a siege mound against it. By the way that he came, By the same shall he return; And he shall not come into this city,' Says the LORD. 'For I will defend this city, to save it For My own sake and for My servant David's sake.'"*

Hezekiah appealed for covenant justice. He got it by praying against his enemy and corporate salvation manifested for Jerusalem. Christian culture today has fostered an atmosphere of unsanctified mercy where there is little justice because it teaches us not to pray against people! Tradition makes the Word of God of no effect. Without accessing the Throne for justice, the church has no hope of bringing an end-time witness.

Corporate salvation comes when we pray against the enemy and remind God of His covenant of mercy which is a two-edged sword where edge one cuts away our sin for personal salvation but edge two cuts off the enemy so that our nation or city can be saved. In this passage Jerusalem faced one Sennacherib but the church faces many united by a common bond of, *"Let us break their bonds in pieces and cast away their cords from us."* Sennacherib's has modern counterparts that often wage war against today's church. Isis, the ACLU and legislators of abortion and homosexuality are some of them. Initially our laws reflected biblical values. Under the assault of the enemy, laws are being changed. European nations have yielded. Canadian laws are beginning to change as well. American leaders, judges and governors of states are caving. And the voice of the Church is silent! Imagine born again pastors standing up to unite homosexual couples in **holy** matrimony. Laws are slowly being passed that would make it "discriminatory" (and lawsuit-worthy) for them to say no. Mercy, compassion and salvation should be offered to individuals where possible. But the church needs to begin taking a stand in prayer. Like the false prophet of Acts 13 blocking Paul's entry to the harvest, only the Hand of the Lord can remove the adversary. Sodom and Gomorrah stand as an example of God's judicial action. Rome stands as another historical example. If the church does not rise and begin to call for covenantal justice we will forfeit our nation as it is filled with iniquity by a modern day Sennacherib bent on utter destruction.

Because Hezekiah prayed, God responded with covenant mercy, and salvation came to the land. Isaiah 37:36-38 records God's action against Sennacherib:

> *Then the angel of the LORD went out, and killed in the camp of the Assyrians one hundred and eighty-five thousand; and when people arose early in the morning, there were the corpses – all dead. So Sennacherib king of Assyria departed and went away, returned home, and remained at Nineveh. Now it came to pass, as he was worshiping in the house of Nisroch his god, that Adrammelech and Sharezer his sons struck him down with the sword; and they escaped into the land of Ararat. Then Esarhaddon his son reigned in his place.*

Salvation comes corporately when the church tugs the rope and opens the door of justice. Jesus offers us the full measure of His covenant for those who are willing to walk in faith and call forth corporate salvation. We either move in this dimension or eventually we will lose our nation. The choice is at the feet of each individual who names the Name of Christ. The Jesus of Revelation is judging and making war. Why have we settled in comfort with Jesus the Savior in the gospels? When the Holy Spirit moves to advance us and we choose to resist His promptings and settle in comfort, we always forfeit our purpose in God to the next generation!

Justice itself is not about
Revenge or retribution,
But it's about salvation's plan,
And sin's due execution.

Jayne Houghton

Chapter 3

What is Truth?

George Wishart (1513-1546), an early Scottish reformer and mentor to John Knox, had a long standing battle with David Beaton, Cardinal and Archbishop of St. Andrews, Scotland. Wishart was banned from preaching in St. Andrews and suffered several attempts on his life. He was captured and sentenced to be burned at the stake in 1546. The Cardinal placed soft cushions in the Tower for his invited guests to view the death of his enemy. His hands were tied, a rope circled his neck, and sacks of gunpowder were placed around him. As the fire was lit the gun powder blew up but Wishart remained alive long enough to declare justice on Cardinal Beaton. Wishart proclaimed the man who proudly watched his death would die in that place shortly. In three short months Cardinal Beaton was killed in the same palace.[4] Jesus brought justice. The more we read church history the more we find examples of Jesus the Judge manifesting covenant justice consistently and overwhelmingly. Only preaching a "seeker-sensitive" gospel could hide this Jesus from a generation.

Pilate was forced to examine Jesus in order to administrate Roman justice. His encounter with Jesus reveals much about the issue of biblical truth. John 18:33-38 states,

---

4. Deer, Jack. *Surprised By the Voice of God.* Grand Rapids, MI: Zonderan Publishing House, 1996. 72.

Then Pilate entered the Praetorium again, called Jesus, and said to Him, "Are You the King of the Jews?" Jesus answered him, "Are you speaking for yourself on this, or did others tell you this about Me?" Pilate answered "Am I a Jew? Your own nation and the chief priests have delivered You to me. What have You done?" Jesus answered, "My kingdom is not of this world. If My kingdom were of this world, My servants would fight, so that I should not be delivered to the Jews; but now My kingdom is not from here." Pilate therefore said to Him, "Are You a king then?" Jesus answered, "You say rightly that I am a king. For this cause I was born, and for this cause I have come into the world, that I should bear witness to the truth. Everyone who is of the truth hears My voice." Pilate said to Him, "What is truth?" And when he had said this, he went out again to the Jews, and said to them, "I find no fault in Him at all."

Jesus makes it plain that one of the primary reasons He came into the world was to *"bear witness to the truth."* His plumbline statement is, *"Everyone who is of the truth hears My voice."* The issue of Jesus bearing witness to the truth and our responsibility for what to do with that truth unfolds from Matthew 12:14-21. Jesus was very pointed in warning His followers not to make Him known because He had an assignment that had to be fulfilled. That assignment involved the primary theme of truth as a standard for justice. Jesus had to take truth and justice to victory. The justice to victory of Matthew 12 is, in Greek, **kree-sis** to **nee-kos. Kree-sis** means 'a decision by a judge, the judgment denotes the notion expressed by the verbal stem, i.e. a verdict, sentence, decision in battle.'[5] We should ask, what level of

5. Kittel, Gerhard. "What Is Truth?" *Theological Dictionary of the New Testament.* Vol. III. Grand Rapids, MO. WM. B. Eerdman's Publishing Company, 1965. 941.

victory is intimated by the Greek word **nee-kos**? Since **nee-kos** is used only four times in the New Testament, the passage where it most appears is in 1 Corinthians 15, which gives us an idea of the strength of this word.

We are told in verses 54-57: *"So when this corruptible has put on incorruption, and this mortal has put on immortality, then shall be brought to pass the saying that is written: 'Death is swallowed up in victory (**nee-kos**). O Death, where is your sting? O Hades, where is your victory?(**nee-kos**)' The sting of death is sin, and the strength of sin is the law. But thanks be to God, who gives us the victory (**nee-kos**) through our Lord Jesus Christ."*

It is obvious that Jesus' mission of taking justice to utter and complete victory had a dimension to it that left nothing out. It was complete. It was total. We have access to the court of heaven in Christ. When Jesus referred to this assignment, He quoted from Isaiah. To be absolutely accurate we have to go to the original source of Isaiah and look at it there. Isaiah 42:1-4 says:

> *Behold! My Servant whom I uphold, My Elect One in whom My soul delights! I have put My Spirit upon Him; He will bring forth justice to the Gentiles. He will not cry out, Nor raise His voice, Nor cause His voice to be heard in the street. A bruised reed He will not break, And smoking flax He will not quench; He will bring forth **justice for truth.** He will not fail nor be discouraged, Till He has **established justice in the earth**; And the coastlands shall wait for His law.*

Verse 3 is of great interest when it says, *"He will bring forth **justice for truth**."* The Hebrew word for justice is the word **mish-pawt** and for truth it is **eh-meth**. The New Testament definition of justice would be, 'an administrative decision or judicial decree to utterly vanquish the enemy.' The Old Testament would be 'a prophetic proclamation establishing God's moral standard by judgment.' The best dictionary for the Bible is always the Bible. Context determines meaning. Verses 4-6 state:

> *He will not fail nor be discouraged, Till He has established justice in the earth; And the coastlands shall wait for His law. Thus says God the LORD, Who created the heavens and stretched them out, Who spread forth the earth and that which comes from it, Who gives breath to the people on it, And spirit to those who walk on it: "I, the LORD, have called You in righteousness, And will hold Your hand; I will keep You and give You as a covenant to the people, As a light to the Gentiles."*

God gave Jesus as a Covenant guaranteeing access to establish His truth through biblical justice. Through the Lord Jesus we have the right to ask, claim, or demand biblical covenantal justice as a means of salvation. Why did Mordecai Ham get this a hundred years ago so that what was routine in his services is hard to comprehend let alone reproduce today? The church is stuck in the mentality of extending personal mercy. They have yet to be awakened to the judicial side of the Davidic covenant. David understood his covenant of mercy applied in war. Hezekiah understood the covenant of mercy applied in war. Mordecai Ham understood the covenant applied in war. How did we become so passive? Our generation is full of ministers who limit the gospel to personal salvation. If the church ever embraces the fullness of their covenant and begins to pray as Hezekiah prayed a new standard of righteousness will emerge in the land and God's Hand will be seen establishing the fear of the Lord and bringing a measure of salvation for which Jesus died. Why should demons destroy our land by filling the nation with iniquity so it has to be judged before we get the harvest?

Isaiah tells us in 42:3 that all justice originates in truth but when we look at Ephesians we realize that one of the primary assignments of the church is to stand up and proclaim the standard of truth from which justice comes. The book of Ephesians is really the New Testament Joshua and Joshua's job was very clear. His job was to turn a prophetic promise into a physical reality. In order to turn that prophetic promise for land into a physical reality he had to follow the God-given path to fulfillment. In Joshua 1:8-9 he was told, *"This Book of the Law shall not depart from your mouth, but you shall meditate in it day and night, that you may observe to do according to all that is written in it. For then you will make your way prosperous, and then you will have good success. Have I not commanded you? Be strong and of good courage; do not be afraid, nor be dismayed, for the LORD your God is with you wherever you go."* Joshua, in order to bring a prophetic promise into reality had to do it by consistently speaking the Word into his heart. The truth of God's Word is seed that takes root in the soil of our lives and when initiated by the Holy Spirit we can speak it forth from our lips with all of heaven to back it up.

Ephesians reveals a heavenly conflict over arenas of truth. Ephesians 3:8-12 declares the purpose for the church,

> *To me, who am less than the least of all the saints, this grace was given, that I should preach among the Gentiles the unsearchable riches of Christ, and to make all people see what is the fellowship of the mystery, which from the beginning of the ages has been hidden in God who created all things through Jesus Christ; to the intent that now the manifold wisdom of God might be made known by the church to the principalities and powers in the heavenly places, according to the eternal purpose which He accomplished in Christ Jesus our Lord, in whom we have boldness and access with confidence through faith in Him.*

Principalities and powers really administrate the kingdom of darkness and they do it through deception. They have their own brand of truth. When a deceived person reads our Constitution they look for license to live their destructive life-style any way they want and are driven to throw off all biblical restraints. When our forefathers established our land they understood that sin could destroy it, so they made destructive sin like homosexuality illegal.

Principalities and powers work hard to deceive people into believing that equal access under the law means they are entitled to freedom to exercise their lifestyle in whatever way they want. Demons proclaim homosexuality a "civil right" and principalities and powers advance that demonic truth. The church, however, has another standard of truth – God's revealed Word. Homosexuality, like all sin, is a choice. And choosing to practice it has consequences. God discriminates against sin and He judges it. We know our God is the same yesterday, today and forever, so we know that judgment can fall on an entire nation. So should the church let sin destroy the nation?

The Bible sets forth the standard of righteousness upon which justice is based. We can access a heavenly court for justice based on God's moral standard. One of the greatest wars against our nation has taken place in the legal arena by deceived individuals who have worked to "interpret" the Constitution so Americans could abort unwanted children. They have shouted, whispered and reasoned demonic rhetoric to the people and defined it as 'tolerance.' The church has access to God's justice based on His moral truth. The problem is we have not used it. Sennacherrib is loose in the land and we have not demanded covenant justice! God did not blink in killing 185,000 for Hezekiah. Why would He blink in removing deceived leaders for the church?

In Matthew 12, Jesus emphatically quotes Isaiah 42:1-3 and then He summarizes verse 6 by stating, in Matthew 12:21, *"And in His name*

Gentiles will trust." But the entirety of Isaiah 42:6 says, *"I, the LORD, have called You in righteousness, And will hold Your hand; I will keep You and give You as a covenant to the people, As a light to the Gentiles..."*

Justice to Victory in Matthew 12 has a particular application in Ephesians. In reading the epistles we often neglect Paul's pedigree as an Old Testament scholar and fail to apply the epistles from an Old Testament mindset, therefore missing a major application. Ephesians presents the pinnacle revelation of God's purpose for the New Testament church. Setting Ephesians in its Old Testament theological context imparts a whole new importance concerning the issue of justice and truth. Ephesians adds understanding through application. The entire theme of the book of Ephesians is the church rising to the fullness of Christ. After tracing this thread through Ephesians and looking at the church in its current condition, the most casual observers would have to agree we are not even at half-measure let alone fullness.

In Ephesians 1:15-23 Paul prays for the condition of the church and that we will get an understanding of the full measure of what Jesus bought and paid for which includes guaranteeing Throne-Room access to institute justice for truth. It says,

> *Therefore I also, after I heard of your faith in the Lord Jesus and your love for all the saints, do not cease to give thanks for you, making mention of you in my prayers: that the God of our Lord Jesus Christ, the Father of glory, may give to you the spirit of wisdom and revelation in the knowledge of Him, the eyes of your understanding being enlightened; that you may know what is the hope of His calling, what are the riches of the glory of His inheritance in the saints, and what is the exceeding greatness of His power toward us who believe, according to the working of His mighty power which He worked in Christ when He raised Him from the dead and seated Him at His right hand in the*

heavenly places, far above all principality and power and might and dominion, and every name that is named, not only in this age but also in that which is to come. And He put all things under His feet, and gave Him to be head over all things to the church, which is His body, the fullness of Him who fills all in all.

The interesting part from Paul's prayer in Ephesians 1 is his last line where he gives biblical definition to the church. Paul's definition is very clearly one where God's truth has been made victorious and he describes the church as the *"...body of Jesus, the fullness of Him who fills all in all."* That in itself is a transformational view of who we are and what is available. This is the theme that continues all the way through the letter. In chapter 2:22 we are told, *"...in whom you also are being built together for a habitation of God in the Spirit."* Fullness consistently appears as the thread that runs throughout the book of Ephesians. In chapter 3:14-21, the second Priestly prayer for the church emerges. Verses 18 and 19 are abundantly clear in continuing this thread, praying that we *"...may be able to comprehend with all the saints what is the width and length and depth and height – to know the love of Christ which passes knowledge; that you may be filled with all the fullness of God."* In chapter 4 we are told the entire purpose of the five-fold ministry of apostles, prophets, evangelists, pastors and teachers is to bring the church to a place where, verse 13 is a reality, *"...we all come to the unity of the faith and the knowledge of the Son of God, to a perfect man, to the measure of the stature of the fullness of Christ."*

In Ephesians 5:18 we are exhorted, *"And do not be drunk with wine, in which is dissipation; but be filled with the Spirit..."* In chapter 6 we are encouraged in verses 10 and following to put on the whole armor of God so we can intercede for victory. Once again, the theme of fullness carries through to the end. It is impossible to read the book of

Ephesians and not realize Jesus Himself not only bought and paid for salvation but has an expectation that we walk in the fullness of the ascended seated Judge of all the earth!

The entire purpose of the armor of God, in Ephesians 6, according to verses 13 through 18, is revealed to us:

> *Therefore take up the whole armor of God, that you may be able to withstand in the evil day, and having done all, to stand. Stand therefore, having girded your waist with truth, having put on the breastplate of righteousness, and having shod your feet with the preparation of the gospel of peace; above all, taking the shield of faith with which you will be able to quench all the fiery darts of the wicked one. And take the helmet of salvation, and the sword of the Spirit, which is the word of God; praying always with all prayer and supplication in the Spirit, being watchful to this end with all perseverance and supplication for all the saints-*

The Apostle Paul understood that the armor of God had a purpose and that purpose was to take the truth and through intercession call for God's Hand moving to establish that standard of truth. The thread that runs through Ephesians compares and contrasts who rules. Jesus made a show of principalities and powers and paid the price to put them under our feet, according to Ephesians 1:22, *"And He put all things under His feet, and gave Him to be head over all things to the church."*

Ephesians presents a church charged with the responsibility of establishing God's moral standard and bringing His justice into any situation where we encounter injustice. Chapter 3 raises the question of who rules. Demons rule through deceived leaders, when the church neglects to demand Throne-Room justice! Supreme Court Justices who protect homosexual marriage open the church to lawsuits for discriminating against homosexuals by refusing to marry them. God discriminates against sin. He judges it. He killed everyone in Sodom and Gomorrah. Demand covenant justice upon errant judges! At Holy Spirit promptings may we declare what God decrees!

Jesus bought and paid for access to victorious justice based on the truth of biblical moral standards. (He took *Justice to Victory*). We have a voice before the throne. Let's use it!

In Luke 19:11-14 Jesus taught a parable that applies when He said:

> *Now as they heard these things, He spoke another parable, because he was near Jerusalem and because they thought the kingdom of God would appear immediately. Therefore He said: "A certain nobleman went into a far country to receive for himself a kingdom and to return. So he called ten of his servants, delivered to them ten minas, and said to them, 'Do business till I come.' But his citizens hated him, and sent a delegation after him, saying, 'We will not have this man to reign over us.'"*

This parable highlights the dysfunction of His "citizens." The problem with the "citizens" was that they refused to allow the king to rule and since the king did not rule over them he could not rule through them.

This parable reveals that one primary purpose of the church is to establish and call forth victorious Kingly justice. Apparently the church has to prove to principalities and powers that Jesus rules – not them! That proof apparently only emerges as we are led into unjust situations where we have a choice of exactly how to respond. God expects us to call forth covenant justice, where we make a stand and put a demand on the covenant. Shadrach, Meshach, and Abed-Nego mentally prepared to meet such a challenge. They refused to bow to an idol. They were thrown in the fire. Truth prevailed and they were delivered.

One question worth asking is how does God feel when He looks at a culture and finds that there is no justice? Isaiah 59 describes the Lord's reaction when He looks at a culture and sees no justice. Isaiah 59:14-15 states, *"Justice is turned back, And righteousness stands afar off; For truth is fallen in the street, And equity cannot enter. So truth fails, And he who departs from evil makes himself a prey. Then the LORD saw it, and it displeased Him That there was no justice."* When Jesus looks at a culture and sees there is no justice He is displeased, which means it is evil in His eyes. When the church has covenant access to divine justice and refuses to execute it, then it is actually enabling evil. Jesus' response in Isaiah 59 was to put on the armor and through intercession subjugate the enemy just as Paul taught in the book of Ephesians. Isaiah 42 declares that once a biblical moral standard has been erased from a culture it is exceedingly difficult to reestablish but not impossible. The question is, can we empower a generation of believers to learn their covenant and birth justice based in biblical truth? Jesus has made everything available that we need. The question is, Are we willing to invest the time and go through the boot camp so we can graduate and help raise a generation who is committed to manifesting the justice of God? If we will, nations can be saved.

From justice to victory...
May this phrase be plain to see.
Bought and paid for on the cross.
To be reluctant...what a loss!

Jayne Houghton

Chapter 4

Justice by Blood Covenant

How can an average person who works a job and attends church on Sunday access God's justice? Albert Stokes, the father of an acquaintance, was just such a man. His daughter Norelle writes:

> *My parents and I had been attending a charismatic church for a couple of years in the mid 1970s when the male churchgoer who had been presiding over the communion was exposed as a practicing homosexual. The pastor, knowing this, still allowed the male homosexual to preside over the communion; i.e. as in give the communion message, pray over the emblems and break the bread. My father spoke to the pastor and challenged him that the homosexual should not be allowed to continue to do this as homosexuality is an abomination and it would bring God's judgment on the pastor and the church. The pastor chose to ignore my father's warning. Two years later the pastor suffered a fatal heart attack and died while he was preaching behind the pulpit!*

Albert Stokes in a few short sentences confronted a pastor who made peace with evil. God did the rest. Justice was done! Albert, as an average hard-working family man, made a choice not to be silent and became an agent of divine justice. In some circumstances, God is waiting on us. The boldness to confront will grow proportionally with our understanding of blood covenant!

It is impossible to fully comprehend God's heart for justice outside of the context of biblical blood covenant. When Abram was complaining in Genesis 15:1-8 about the fact that God had promised but had not given him a son, the Lord came to him in verse 5 and said, *"'Look now toward heaven, and count the stars if you are able to number them.' And He said to him, 'So shall your descendants be.'"* Abram believed God and the Lord counted it unto him as righteousness. But Abram still had a non-performance issue with God for what had already been promised. Abram asked how he could KNOW that God would actually perform what He promised. Over time the promise lost its value and Abram was asking for concrete assurance. He asked for something stronger than just words. Most of us would not have the courage to confront God with the potential unfulfillment of His word, but Abram did and perhaps in this place he earns his nickname as the *"Father of all them that believe."* A covenant is a two-way street. Once this covenant was given, God could demand to know Abraham's commitment. God's demand to know appears in Genesis 22. God demanded to KNOW that Abram was as wholeheartedly committed as He had been. Since God was willing to sacrifice His Son – He demanded Abram sacrifice his. This is true blood covenant. We would do well to note that when we approach God demanding covenant, the day may well come when He approaches us with a parallel demand. Perhaps the condition of the church today, in its failure to execute biblical justice lies in an underdeveloped understanding of blood covenant. Perhaps we never taught a generation to fully embrace God's covenant and expect the same responses Abraham got. We cannot expect God's fullness if we are not willing to give God our fullness. When Abram put a demand on a covenant promise – God met him according to covenant. Biblical justice is codified for all generations in the Abrahamic covenant!

A biblical blood covenant has eight primary steps to a new

beginning. The first step is one person has to be the initiator by asking for it. Abraham started the process by asking for an iron-clad guarantee that God would do what He promised! Abraham asked in Genesis 15:8 and God responded in verse 9, *"So He said to him, 'Bring Me a three-year-old heifer, a three-year-old female goat, a three-year-old ram, a turtledove, and a young pigeon.''* Abram cut the animals in two because entering a blood covenant is a promise unto death for each individual participant. Standing in the midst of death to complete each step signifies this. Each person would vow pointing to the dead animal declaring, "God do so to me and more if I ever break this covenant." Every blood covenant had both a blessing and a curse. The blessing offered accessibility to all the assets of your covenant partner whenever you needed them. The key definition being that of need! And if your covenant partner called on those assets and you refused then you could expect to be cut in half. Blood covenants were serious. They would become the foundation for all biblical justice.

In Jeremiah 34:18-20, God proclaims the fate of men who break a blood covenant. It says:

> *And I will give the men who have transgressed My covenant, who have not performed the words of the covenant which they made before Me, when they cut the calf in two and passed between the parts of it – the princes of Judah, the princes of Jerusalem, the eunuchs, the priests, and all the people of the land who passed between the parts of the calf – I will give them into the hand of their enemies and into the hand of those who seek their life. Their dead bodies shall be for meat for the birds of the heaven and the beasts of the earth.*

God keeps His blood covenants and expects us to do the same. Matthew 27:25 records the Jewish people breaking a blood covenant,

"And all the people answered and said, 'His blood be on us and on our children.'" The fruit of breaking blood covenant can be read in the Josephus account of what Titus and the Roman Legions executed in A.D. 70 as they conquered Jerusalem. Jesus wept over Jerusalem and prophesied justice. God is as serious today about blood covenant as He was two thousand years ago.

The second step and primary reason for making a blood covenant was the reading of the assets. The doubling of your assets based on the wealth of your covenant partner was a laudable goal. Deuteronomy 28:1-3 provides an introduction to the blessing of blood covenant assets:

> *Now it shall come to pass, if you diligently obey the voice of the LORD your God, to observe carefully all His commandments which I command you today, that the LORD your God will set you high above all nations of the earth. And all these blessings shall come upon you and overtake you, because you obey the voice of the LORD your God: "Blessed shall you be in the city, and blessed shall you be in the country."*

Verses 11-13 continue the blessing

> *And the LORD will grant you plenty of goods, in the fruit of your body, in the increase of your livestock, and in the produce of your ground, in the land of which the LORD swore to your fathers to give you. The LORD will open to you His good treasure, the heavens, to give the rain to your land in its season, and to bless all the work of your hand. You shall lend to many nations, but you shall not borrow. And the LORD will make you the head and not the tail; you shall be above only, and not be beneath, if you heed the commandments of the LORD your God, which I command you today, and are careful to observe them.*

Failure to abide by the standard of a blood covenant brought verses 15-16 into manifestation, *"But it shall come to pass, if you do not obey the voice of the LORD your God, to observe carefully all His commandments and His statutes which I command you today, that all these curses will come upon you and overtake you: Cursed shall you be in the city, and cursed shall you be in the country."*

The blessing of a blood covenant was guaranteed access to everything your covenant partner possessed if you needed it. The primary motivation for entering blood covenant was that at the minimum it would double your available assets. God made a blood covenant in response to Abram's request to know. Blood covenant was the result of man asking for a guarantee that God would do what He promised! Everything God possessed became available to Abram and God gained the right to ask for everything Abram possessed. In Genesis 22 God asked for his son Isaac. Step #2 in blood covenant was always pleasant initially as each individual learned what they gained in the reading of the assets. The real price of covenant came when a demand was placed on those assets. Are we prepared to answer God's covenant request for everything? If we want everything from God, then we better be!

Step #3 in a blood covenant is evidenced in 1 Samuel 18:1-4, which states:

> *And it was so, when he had finished speaking to Saul, that the soul of Jonathan was knit to the soul of David, and Jonathan loved him as his own soul. Saul took him that day, and would not let him go home to his father's house anymore. Then Jonathan and David made a covenant, because he loved him as his own soul. And Jonathan took off the robe that was on him and gave it to David, with his armor, even to his sword and his bow and his belt.*

Step #3 in blood covenant was always a major blessing because it involved an exchange of weapons and the pledge that if you found yourself in battle you had every right to draw upon the full ability of your blood covenant partner who was obligated to join you in that war. Justice began here. This is an element of blood covenant that is clearly lost in the church today. Paul warned Timothy about perilous times in the last days when men would be "covenant breakers." If we break our covenant with each other, we break our covenant with God. We cannot afford to forfeit covenant protections in the last days: we must keep covenant with each other.

One example of covenantal intervention in battle through prayer is in Joshua 10:9-14 which says:

> *Joshua therefore came upon them suddenly, having marched all night from Gilgal. So the LORD routed them before Israel, killed them with a great slaughter at Gibeon, chased them along the road that goes to Beth Horon, and struck them down as far as Azekah and Makkedah. And it happened, as they fled before Israel and were on the descent of Beth Horon, that the LORD cast down large hailstones from heaven on them as far as Azekah, and they died. There were more who died from the hailstones than those whom the children of Israel killed with the sword. Then Joshua spoke to the LORD in the day when the LORD delivered up the Amorites before the children of Israel, and he said in the sight of Israel: "Sun, stand still over Gibeon; And Moon, in the Valley of Aijalon." So the sun stood still, And the moon stopped, Till the people had revenge [took covenant vengeance] upon their enemies. Is this not written in the Book of Jasher? So the sun stood still in the midst of heaven, and did not hasten to go down for about a whole day. And there has been no day like that, before it or after it that the LORD heeded the voice of a man; for the LORD fought for Israel.*

When Christian nations go to war, they should make sure they have not violated covenant or God could become their enemy. By covenant God aids in killing the enemy but when covenant is broken wrath falls on the violating party!

One of the primary reasons people entered blood covenant was for aid in war. Joshua understood that and executed covenant. Most Christians today are completely unaware of any such privilege and never ask. Joshua appealed to God for covenant justice and God answered his prayer. Then God honored covenant by killing more with hailstones than the Israelites did militarily. Joshua executed covenant vengeance. The Hebrew says they took covenant vengeance. Covenant vengeance is a manifestation of divine justice. The Bible says, "*Vengeance is Mine, I will repay*." It is the solemn declaration that God is a God of justice, He functions on principles of justice and His blood covenant gives us access to His justice. Joshua accessed and took it.

The New Testament church today, is tragically passive in the face of evil. There is very little understanding of covenant justice and God's willingness to stand up for the church to do what only He can. When King David found himself in war he called for the full capabilities of his covenant Partner. Today most believers are utterly unaware of what is available. We do not even see the church asking for covenant justice, let alone putting a demand on the full capability of God in our behalf. We serve the God who stopped the rotation of the planets in order to give justice to His people. He is the same yesterday, today and forever! Through biblical ignorance of blood covenant, have generations of Christians forfeited moving the Hand of the Lord upon their enemies and gaining a victory which scripture promises? Surely for the generation who is charged with harvesting the nations, a restoration of covenant vengeance is essential. In preparing those who would go forth into the nations to face a persistent and determined enemy, we have an obligation to establish access to Jesus the Judge. Will the demonized radical Islamists conquer the world or will the church move the hand of the LORD to destroy them and free multitudes under their influence, setting millions free for a harvest?

When Elijah faced the prophets of Baal he had no problem calling on his covenant Partner to rain fire from heaven. When God answered, all the people said, we will serve the Lord. Elijah promptly executed the prophets of Baal. When Elisha was mocked by youth, he pronounced covenant vengeance and bears came out of the woods and mauled 42 perpetrators. Covenant vengeance has not changed from Old Testament to New. The Apostle Paul invoked a curse in 2 Corinthians on all those who preach another Jesus or another gospel. By elevating "turn the other cheek" out of the context in which it was taught, we have robbed the church of covenant justice! The God of justice is every bit as available to us by blood covenant as He has been to His people throughout scripture. "Turn the other cheek" is a powerful weapon but it does not always apply! The question is, Do we know when to turn the other cheek and when to initiate covenant justice? Once we learn justice is an assignment, the next challenge is to live in such a manner as to **qualify** to put a demand on that justice. The church can no longer afford to be ignorant of the blood covenant when godless judges and politicians sweep away with one decision or one vote what generations of Godly Americans died for. The time for covenant vengeance is here! It is only a declaration away!

In step #4 blood covenant earns its name by both parties shedding blood. Genesis 17:9-11 says, *"And God said to Abraham: 'As for you, you shall keep My covenant, you and your descendants after you throughout their generations. This is My covenant which you shall keep, between Me and you and your descendants after you: Every male child among you shall be circumcised; and you shall be circumcised in the flesh of your foreskins, and it shall be a sign of the covenant between Me and you.'"* Abram had to cut the animals in two as a demonstration and then God put a demand on him to shed blood for this covenant in his own body through circumcision. The reason why they call it a blood covenant is because each party sheds blood. The animals that Abram cut in two were just a sign of what God was willing to do at a future date when He Himself would shed His own blood for the redemption of mankind.

In step #5 there was a name change, as if each party adopted the other. You took on a measure of your covenant partner's name and they took on part of your name. In Genesis 17:5-7 we find:

> *No longer shall your name be called Abram, but your name shall be Abraham; for I have made you a father of many nations. I will make you exceedingly fruitful; and I will make nations of you, and kings shall come from you. And I will establish My covenant between Me and you and your descendants after you in their generations, for an everlasting covenant, to be God to you and your descendants after you.*

God became known as the God of Abraham and Abram took one of the syllables of Elohim into his name. The "ha" of Elohim was added to Abram and he became Abraham.

In step #6 all the future generations are covered in the covenant so the covenant that you enter not only impacts you, but it impacts all your future generations. They benefit as it continues in their lives. Genesis 17:15-19 states:

> *Then God said to Abraham, "As for Sarai your wife, you shall not call her name Sarai, but Sarah shall be her name. And I will bless her and also give you a son by her; then I will bless her, and she shall be a*

mother of nations; kings of peoples shall be from her." Then Abraham fell on his face and laughed, and said in his heart, "Shall a child be born to a man who is one hundred years old? And shall Sarah, who is ninety years old, bear a child?" And Abraham said to God, "Oh, that Ishmael might live before You!" Then God said: "No, Sarah your wife shall bear you a son, and you shall call his name Isaac; I will establish My covenant with him for an everlasting covenant, and with his descendants after him."

Abraham got his son and the blood covenant was the guarantee that God would perform the miracle and bring him a son to establish future generations and a biblical culture. The covenant includes our future generations!

Step #7 and #8 flow very closely together as one becomes the platform for the other. Every blood covenant ended with a celebratory meal. Step #8 included declaratory oaths or promises of covenant. Genesis 26:28-31 states:

But they said, "We have certainly seen that the LORD is with you. So we said, 'Let there now be an oath between us, between you and us; and let us make a covenant with you, that you will do us no harm, since we have not touched you, and since we have done nothing to you but good and have sent you away in peace. You are now the blessed of the Lord.'" So he made them a feast, and they ate and drank. Then they arose early in the morning and swore an oath with one another; and Isaac sent them away, and they departed from him in peace.

Every covenant was ended with a covenant celebration and promises! Today the demonstration of that covenant meal is communion. Every communion should include the declaring of covenant promises. According to 1 Corinthians 11 every time we partake of it we are declaring blood covenant just as verses 23 through 25 state:

> *For I received from the Lord that which I also delivered to you: that the Lord Jesus on the same night in which He was betrayed took bread; and when He had given thanks, He broke it and said, "Take, eat; this is My body which is broken for you; do this in remembrance of Me." In the same manner He also took the cup after supper, saying, "This cup is the new covenant in My blood. This do, as often as you drink it, in remembrance of Me."*

Every time we take communion we declare the fact that we have a blood covenant with God. The eighth step was the promise comprising a new beginning. We always seem to end it right there and it never goes any further. The power of the blood covenant is the power to put a demand on God for biblical justice and a new beginning when needed. In order for us to enjoy the full measure of the blessing we must choose to live within the boundaries of covenant. Deuteronomy 4:37-40 essentially states this:

> *And because He loved your fathers, therefore He chose their descendants after them; and He brought you out of Egypt with His Presence, with His mighty power, driving out from before you nations greater and mightier than you, to bring you in, to give you their land as an inheritance, as it is this day. Therefore know this day, and consider it in your heart, that the LORD Himself is God in heaven above and on the earth beneath; there is no other. You shall therefore keep His statutes and His commandments which I command you today, that it may go well with you and with your children after you, and that you*

may prolong your days in the land which the LORD your God is giving you for all time.

Biblical blood covenant has astounding blessings revealed in Deuteronomy 28:1-14 which America enjoyed through the 1960s. Deuteronomy 28:15-68 has verses which describe what has transpired since. The judgments for disobedience continue to manifest in ever greater measures as culture departs from God's righteous standards. For generations Americans served God and stayed within the boundaries He proclaimed. Legal barriers barring homosexuality proclaimed the willingness of Americans to stay within biblical boundaries. That willingness qualified us for receiving the blessing of God. But the determination of judges and politicians to bless same-sex marriage declares the opposite. This can do nothing but invite the judgment of God and move us toward the destruction of the culture. What are the righteous to do? No people can keep their land and allow it to be filled with iniquity at the same time. Moses was faced with wayward leaders who were determined to destroy him. He asked God to do a new thing, something that had not been seen before. Moses stood on his covenant. Numbers 16:15 states, "*Then Moses was very angry, and said to the LORD, 'Do not respect their offering. I have not taken one donkey from them, nor have I hurt one of them.'*" Verses 28-32 state,

Then Moses said: "By this you shall know that the LORD has sent me to do all these works, for I have not done them of my own will. If these men die naturally like all men, or if they are visited by the common fate of all men, then the LORD has not sent me. But if the LORD creates a new thing, and the earth opens its mouth and swallows them up with all that belongs to them, and they go down alive into the pit, then you will understand that these men have rejected the LORD." Then it came to pass, as he finished speaking all these words, that the ground split apart under them and the earth opened its mouth and swallowed them up, with their households and all the men with Korah, with all their goods.

Moses knew how to appeal to God for covenant justice and he got it. Praying for God to intervene is not new. George Washington continued the tradition of the Pilgrims. America's first president and esteemed Founding Father was a strong believer and a man of prayer. William J Federer in *America's God and Country* quotes:

> *Henry Muhlenberg,...one of the founders of the Lutheran church in America,...said, "I heard a fine example today, namely, that His Excellency General Washington rode around among his army yesterday and admonished each and every one to fear God, to put away the wickedness that has set in and become so general, and to practice the Christian virtues. From all appearances, this gentleman does not belong to the so-called world and society, for he respects God's Word, believes in the atonement through Christ, and bears himself in humility and gentleness. Therefore, the Lord God has also singularly, yea, marvelously, preserved him from harm in the midst of countless perils, ambuscades, fatigues, etc., and hitherto graciously held him in His hand as a chosen vessel."*[6]

America exists because of God's covenant!

[6.] Federer, William J. *America's God and Country.* Coppell, TX: Fame Publishing, 1994. 641, 643, 645-6.

On August 20, 1778, General Washington wrote to his friend, Brigadier-General Thomas Nelson in Virginia, stating: "The hand of Providence has been so conspicuous in all this [the course of the war] that he must be worse than an infidel that lacks faith, and more wicked that has not gratitude to acknowledge his obligations; but it will be time enough for me to turn Preacher when my present appointment ceases."[7]

As Washington prayed, God dramatically moved in the weather to bring deliverance to his troops and preserve them for a day of victory:

In a bold move, on January 17, 1781, George Washington's southern army, led by General George Morgan, defeated the entire detachment of British Colonel Tarleton's troops at Cowpens. Lord Cornwallis was infuriated and immediately begun pursuing the American troops. He decided to wait the night at the Catawba River, where the American troops had crossed just two hours earlier, but to his distress, a storm began during the night, causing the river to be uncrossable for days. On February 3, Lord Cornwallis nearly overtook the American troops again at the Yadkin River, watching the American troops getting out on the other side. But before they could cross, a sudden flood ran the river over its banks, preventing the British from crossing. On February 13, only a few hours ahead of the British, the American troops crossed the Dan River into Virginia. When the British arrived, again the river had risen, stopping the British from pursuing. British Commander-in-Chief Henry Clinton wrote, explaining the incident: "Here the royal was again stopped by a sudden rise of the waters, which had only just fallen (almost miraculously) to let the enemy over, who could not else have

---

7. Federer, 643.

eluded Lord Cornwallis' grasp, so close was he upon their rear."[8]

Nine months later, "On October 19, 1781... Lord Cornwallis surrendered at Yorktown. General Washington called for a service to give thanksgiving to God."[9] Our country was founded by men who knew how to pray. They put a demand on God for covenant justice! God heard and answered. Should we now forfeit what their blood bought and paid for? George Washington's generation prayed and God answered to start a nation. As I was preparing this manuscript, I heard the Lord say, **"If I answered the Founding Father's prayers to birth a nation, will I not answer your generation's prayers to save it?"** When we pray justice prayers God answers to preserve our nation! Today's Lord Cornwallis', fast upon our rear, are deceived judges and politicians whose Yorktown is just a judicial prayer away – utter it and save the land!

We have a choice in how we pray for the men and women inviting perversion into the nation whether nationally or locally. Supreme Court Justices who support abortion and the homosexual agenda deserve their own encounter with Jesus the Judge! If we as Christians continue to pray ***for*** them then we enable them to stay in position and continue to bring destruction and judgment on the land. If, however, we pray ***against*** them and ask God to have mercy on the nation and remove the perpetrators, then we stand a good chance of stopping the judgment on the land and moving God's Hand upon the perpetrators. God is a God of justice but His justice is by covenant. We have a right to demand covenant justice!

Through intercession the same covenant justice that destroys

---

8. Federer, 645.

9. Federer, 646.

perpetrators can save the land for a harvest. Deuteronomy 9:25-29 gives us this example:

> *Thus I prostrated myself before the LORD; forty days and forty nights I kept prostrating myself, because the LORD had said He would destroy you. Therefore I prayed to the LORD, and said: "O Lord GOD, do not destroy Your people and Your inheritance whom You have redeemed through Your greatness, whom You have brought out of Egypt with a mighty hand. Remember Your servants, Abraham, Isaac, and Jacob; do not look on the stubbornness of this people, or on their wickedness or their sin, lest the land from which You brought us should say, 'Because the LORD was not able to bring them to the land which He promised them, and because He hated them, He has brought them out to kill them in the wilderness.' Yet they are Your people and Your inheritance, whom You brought out by Your mighty power and by Your outstretched arm."*

Moses interceded for the people and stayed the hand of justice in order to keep and gain the full measure of the harvest God promised him, which was bringing the nation to their inheritance. The perpetrators perished in judgment.

Throughout scripture we find examples of covenant justice being executed by God through the appeal of believers in conflict. The time has come for the church to renew their understanding of blood covenant and to draw on the Author of all justice Who is ready to intervene in our behalf. Perhaps the greatest days of the church are ahead, especially if we rise up on the wings of the wind and partner with God in restoring justice in the land.

In 1 Samuel 15:1-3 God tells Saul the following,

Samuel also said to Saul, "The LORD sent me to anoint you king over His people, over Israel. Now therefore, heed the voice of the words of the LORD." Thus says the LORD of hosts: "I will punish what Amalek did to Israel, how he laid wait for him on the way when he came up from Egypt. Now go and attack Amalek, and utterly destroy all that they have, and do not spare them. But kill both man and woman, infant and nursing child, ox and sheep, camel and donkey."

Now what God told Saul to do was pretty radical because in effect He said, "Kill them all, '*...man, woman, infant and nursing child, ox and sheep, camel and donkey.*' Kill them all." The first thing we ask is, "Why? What did they do that merited the utter annihilation of their society?" The answer comes in Deuteronomy 25:17-19 and has a bearing in how we conduct war today. In Deuteronomy 25 we are told in verses 17-19:

Remember what Amalek did to you on the way as you were coming out of Egypt, how he met you on the way and attacked your rear ranks, all the stragglers at your rear, when you were tired and weary; and he did not fear God. Therefore it shall be, when the LORD your God has given you rest from your enemies all around, in the land which the LORD your God is giving you to possess as an inheritance, that you will blot out the remembrance of Amalek from under heaven. You shall not forget.

It seems that when it comes to covenant people God has a standard and that standard is justice. Because Amalek waited until the end of the day and attacked Israel where the women, the children and the aged were congregating, God declared, "I will utterly destroy them from under heaven." As we apply biblical covenantal justice today and as we consider that the spirit of Amalek is alive and well in radical Islam because they attack the innocent continually and consistently, we can project how God feels about that and what covenant vengeance looks like. Covenant justice is the complete annihilation of radical Islam in the earth and any nation that supports or aids them. Failure to take that posture is to surrender to the doctrine of demons. The stated goal of some Middle Eastern leaders is to completely annihilate Israel. There is only one prayer stance that a Christian can take to demand covenant justice on such leaders. There is only one biblical response.

Let the same angel who visited Sennacherib's army visit them. For those who question whether the New Testament God of love still releases judgment according to the Old Testament principle, the answer is in Revelation 16:4-6. It says, *"Then the third angel poured out his bowl on the rivers and springs of water, and they became blood. And I heard the angel of the waters saying: 'You are righteous, O Lord, The One who is and who was and who is to be, Because You have judged these things. For they have shed the blood of saints and prophets, And You have given them blood to drink. For it is their just due.'"*

As the Author of ALL justice, God progressively reveals Himself in scripture. He is Creator, Covenant-keeper to a thousand generations and Author of justice. As the Creator of the heavens and earth, He reserves all justice to Himself, clearly outlining the actions that fill the creation with iniquity, demanding judgment. In Genesis 9:1-9 we are told,

> *So God blessed Noah and his sons, and said to them: "Be fruitful and multiply, and fill the earth. And the fear of you and the dread of you shall be on every beast of the earth, on every bird of the air, on all that move on the earth, and on all the fish of the sea. They are given into your hand. Every moving thing that lives shall be food for you. I have*

given you all things, even as the green herbs. But you shall not eat flesh with its life, that is, its blood. Surely for your lifeblood I will demand a reckoning; from the hand of every beast I will require it, and from the hand of man. From the hand of every man's brother I will require the life of man. Whoever sheds man's blood, By man his blood shall be shed; For in the image of God He made man. And as for you, be fruitful and multiply; Bring forth abundantly in the earth And multiply in it." Then God spoke to Noah and to his sons with him, saying: "And as for Me, behold, I establish My covenant with you and with your descendants after you."

Verse 6 is a strong statement of justice based on the fact that we were created in the image of God and because we were created in the image of God, justice is demanded for every person that sheds innocent blood. Imagine what the accrual of fifty million abortions brings upon a nation. As we look at the God of justice and apply the very first elementary principle revealed, the conclusion is staggering. According to Genesis 9, for those fifty million innocent babies murdered, fifty million adults must die in payment. Are we ready for Genesis 9 justice as prophesied in Revelation?

Preterism is an eschatological view that interprets biblical prophecies (like in Daniel and Revelation) as events which have already happened, and futurism interprets them as future events. Scholars have always recognized, whether Old Testament or New Testament, prophecy has a propensity for both a preterist and futurist fulfillment.[10] In Revelation 6:8, Jesus judges and destroys one-fourth of earth's

---

10. Bullinger, E.W. *Numbers In Scripture.* Grand Rapids, MI: Kregel Publications. 1967. 237-8. Citing the 14th siege Jerusalem: "The whole city was pillaged, 10,000 captives taken, the walls were destroyed, the altar was defiled, ancient manuscripts perished, the fine buildings were burned, and the Jews were forbidden to worship there. This was the Preteritist fulfillment of Daniel's prophecy (ix & xi), and a foreshadowing example of what the Futurist fulfillment will yet be."

population while in Revelation 9 it is one-third, for a total of seven-twelfths. Are we prepared to represent Jesus the Judge? The Jesus of Revelation as Judge of all the earth kills more than He saves!

In Genesis 12:1-3 God extends a covenant to Abram, saying *"Now the LORD had said to Abram: 'Get out of your country, From your kindred And from your father's house, To a land that I will show you. I will make you a great nation; I will bless you And make your name great; And you shall be a blessing. I will bless those who bless you, And I will curse him who curses you; And in you all the families of the earth shall be blessed.'"* The strong judicial component of the Abrahamic covenant arises in verse 3 when God says, *"I will bless those who bless you, And I will curse him who curses you..."* We could say that God's principle of justice is very simple: whatever man does to you, covenant partner Abram, I will do to him. We do not have to read very far to find an application of this principle because in chapter 12:14-17 we are told:

> *So it was, when Abram came into Egypt, that the Egyptians saw the woman, that she was very beautiful. The princes of Pharaoh also saw her and commended her to Pharaoh. And the woman was taken to Pharaoh's house. He treated Abram well for her sake. He had sheep, oxen, male donkeys, male and female servants, female donkeys, and camels. But the LORD plagued Pharaoh and his house with great plagues because of Sarai, Abram's wife.*

Pharaoh found out very quickly that God was willing to intervene to save His covenant people. Covenant justice and covenant vengeance correspond. How nations responded to Israel is how God treated them.

Covenant biblical justice decrees: how you touch God's people is how God touches you. It becomes an important principle as we move through scripture with God revealing to Abraham that his seed will be in

Egypt four hundred years and at the end of that time they will come out. If the principle is consistent, then God will do to Egypt what Egypt has done to the Israelites. From the biblical record we know the Egyptians afflicted the Israelites for a long time, forced them into slavery and made them build cities, but God blessed the Israelites and they prospered anyway. We are told in Exodus 1:9-14:

> *And he said to his people, "Look, the people of the children of Israel are more and mightier than we; come, let us deal wisely with them, lest they multiply, and it happen, in the event of war, that they also join our enemies and fight against us, and so go up out of the land." Therefore they set taskmasters over them to afflict them with their burdens. And they built for Pharaoh supply cities, Pithom and Raamses. But the more they afflicted them, the more they multiplied and grew. And they were in dread of the children of Israel. So the Egyptians made the children of Israel serve with rigor. And they made their lives bitter with hard bondage – in mortar, in brick, and in all manner of service in the field. All their service in which they made them serve was with rigor.*

The closer the time came for Israel's deliverance the more they were afflicted in Egypt. God was even involved in that affliction. Psalm 105:23-25 reveals His Hand, *"Israel also came into Egypt, And Jacob sojourned in the land of Ham. And He increased His people greatly, And made them stronger than their enemies.* ***He turned their heart to hate His people, To deal craftily with His servants."*** This brings up the question, why would God turn the hearts of the Egyptians against His Own people the Israelites? The answer to that question is seen in the principle of "fullness" as it relates to covenant justice.. In order to release an anointing to legally judge all the gods of Egypt, the Egyptians had to **fill the cup of iniquity** in their treatment of the Israelites. This demanded covenantal justice resulting in the freeing of the entire nation. Out of the tragedy of Hitler's actions in World War II came the fulfillment of Isaiah 66:8 and a nation was born in one day – Israel is a nation today because of covenant.

Exodus chapter 2:23-25 reveals this deepening process:

Now it happened in the process of time that the king of Egypt died. Then the children of Israel groaned because of the bondage, and they cried out; and their cry came up to God because of the bondage. So God heard their groaning, and God remembered His covenant with Abraham, with Isaac, and with Jacob. And God looked upon the children of Israel, and God acknowledged them.

The cry for covenant justice, which would result in their freedom would destroy Egypt in judgment. One of the things that Pharaoh did in order to intimidate and forestall the inevitable deliverance is seen in Exodus 1:15-16. This is part of what helped fill the cup of iniquity demanding covenant vengeance when justice was requested. Exodus 1:15-16 says, *"Then the king of Egypt spoke to the Hebrew midwives, of whom the name of one was Shiphrah and the name of the other Puah; and he said, 'When you do the duties of a midwife for the Hebrew women, and see them on the birthstools, if it is a son, then you shall kill him; but if it is a daughter, then she shall live.'"* But the midwives feared God more than the king so they let all the children live. Not to be deterred, Pharaoh made a second intervention. In Exodus 1:22 we are told, *"So Pharaoh commanded all his people, saying, 'Every son who is born you shall cast into the river, and every daughter you shall save alive.'"* An entire generation of Hebrew sons was killed by drowning. The principle of divine justice states, "How you touch Abram is how I will touch you." Eighty years later as Moses was executing justice on all the gods of Egypt we are told in Exodus 12:12, *"For I will pass through the land of Egypt on that night, and will strike all the firstborn in the land of Egypt, both man and beast; and against all the gods of Egypt I will execute judgment: I am the LORD."* When justice is accomplished through judgment, does the covenant principle that God promised Abraham still hold true? The answer is "yes." In Exodus 14:30-31 we are told, *"So the LORD saved Israel that day out of the hand of the Egyptians, and Israel saw the Egyptians dead on the seashore. Thus Israel saw the great work which the LORD had done in Egypt; so the people feared the LORD, and believed the LORD and His servant Moses."*

Just as the Egyptians drowned a generation of Hebrew children, so God drowned the entire Egyptian army in one moment of time. Apparently covenant justice has not changed. There is no difference. It consistently appears in scripture from generation to generation and from Genesis to Revelation. Jesus' heart for justice has been lost generationally. Some teachers have gone so far as to declare there is no more judgment because Jesus took it all on Himself. This view states all judgment fell on Jesus and therefore there is only salvation to be received. To be biblically literate and declare, "There is no more judgment" is astonishing in the light of reading Revelation. The message may sound good in the initial hearing, but the truth of the matter is it does not stand the light of scripture. The covenant principle of justice that God starts in Genesis passes consistently through to the book of Revelation.

When we talk about justice by covenant, we realize that in Exodus 19 God offered the Israelites the priesthood, which they initially accepted, and once they found out what the price was, they agreed together to let Moses pay the price and come back and tell them what God said. In chapter 20 the Ten Commandments were audibly verbally delivered by God from heaven to the Israelites. As God began to interact with covenant Israel, commandments, judgments, and ordinances emerged covering different areas of life. The Ten Commandments governed their personal lives relating to God. The judgments of Exodus 21 through Exodus 24:11 governed their social lives relating to each other. In Exodus 24:12 through 31:18 the ordinances governed their religious lives in approaching God. There is a reason why we are told to study. 2 Timothy 2:15 says, *"Be diligent to present yourself approved to God, a worker who does not need to be ashamed, rightly dividing the word of truth."*

The reason why we have to study or prepare is because the Word has to be rightly divided or rightly interpreted. Galatians 3:10-14 says:

> *For as many as are of the works of the law are under the curse; for it is written, "Cursed is everyone who does not continue in all things which are written in the book of the law, to do them." But that no one is justified by the law in the sight of God is evident, for "The just shall live by faith." Yet the law is not of faith, but "The man who does them shall live by them." Christ has redeemed us from the curse of the law, having become a curse for us (for it is written, "Cursed is everyone who hangs on a tree"), that the blessing of Abraham might come upon the Gentiles in Christ Jesus, that we might receive the promise of the Spirit through faith.*

Without study we might conclude all judgment fell on Jesus and it is not an issue. But as we continue to follow this thread throughout the New Testament we find plenty of places where the same biblical principle still applies.

Abraham saved Sarah's life by accessing the covenant. I wish the church could ask Abimelech to comment on the strength of Abraham's covenant because in Genesis 20:7 he was on the Judicial receiving end.

Maybe *then* we could grasp it! God met Abimelech to kill him and his whole nation if he refused to let Sarah go free! Abimelech learned the strength of God's covenant the hard way!

The result of our religious tradition emphasizing Jesus the Savior has been to hide through neglect the principles of Jesus the Judge. In effect, all of us in church leadership are guilty by silence of the same sin that Jesus rebuked the church at Pergamus for in allowing or tolerating evil in their midst. Many churches have made peace with evil through silence. The only Jesus that most of the American church knows is Jesus the Savior, Who saves **all** of the time. Few of us know Jesus the Judge and have not learned to access the Throne for justice. Church leadership has not educated the Body of Christ about this side of our Savior. A parallel picture of how leadership has educated the saints might be a university that graduates students who never learned to read. When it comes to knowing the Lord Jesus as Judge of all the earth, today's church resembles an illiterate graduating class.

Justice is a foundational principle because it is the very pillar of God's Throne. Because of this neglect, much of the church is not equipped to bring God's response to evil. In some states, pastors cannot refuse to join two men or two women in marriage without risking a discrimination lawsuit. Using the phrase "Mom and Dad" is being disallowed in some public textbooks. Transgender legislation is being signed into law giving schoolchildren the right to use ***either*** the boys or girls bathroom facilities if they "feel like" that gender. But within two weeks of this law passing, a billion dollars was burned up in real estate by devastating fires in my home state. Within thirty days of one state's Supreme Court passing laws allowing homosexual marriage, a freak lightning storm started over 1,700 fires and grew to 2,700 fires where thousands of acres were burned. Is there a connection between anti-biblical laws and these devastating events? God alone knows how much adversity will have to come before legislators see God's Hand!

Where is repentance? Sometimes it is difficult to discern whether a catastrophic event is judgment on the land. But throughout the Word, we see judgment fall when a land continues to increase in iniquity without turning. I recently endured a 5.4 earthquake 6 miles from my house. Many close to the epicenter had significant damage in their homes. As perversion grows in California, earthquakes may increase in frequency and intensity until there is such devastation that a once beautiful land could be an unfit place to live. Saving the land demands a heart-cry for justice on the perpetrators. The church has a responsibility to move the Hand of God and bring justice on those defiling the land.

Galatians 5:16-18 states, *"I say then: Walk in the Spirit, and you shall not fulfill the lust of the flesh. For the flesh lusts against the Spirit, and the Spirit against the flesh; and these are contrary to one another, so that you do not do the things that you wish. But if you are led by the Spirit, you are not under the law."* It is obvious that by walking in the Spirit we are not under the law, but we also know from Matthew 5:17-19 that Jesus did not come to do away with the Law and the Prophets but to fulfill them.

Finally if we look at Romans 3:27-31 we are told:

> *Where is boasting then? It is excluded. By what law? Of works? No, but by the law of faith. Therefore we conclude that a man is justified by faith apart from the deeds of the law. Or is He the God of the Jews only? Is He not also the God of the Gentiles? Yes, of the Gentiles also, since there is one God who will justify the circumcised by faith and the uncircumcised through faith. Do we then make void the law through faith? Certainly not! On the contrary, we establish the law.*

God has never broken a covenant. Jesus did not come to do away with the law but to fulfill it. Christ redeemed us from the curse of the law meaning one violation makes us guilty of all. If we walk in the spirit we fulfill the law. Judgment still comes to violators. Ananias and Sapphira were killed for setting the gold of mammon (love of money) ahead of the Lord. In Revelation 2 the church at Pergamos is warned for tolerating adultery. The law is still God's judicial standard. Some teachers proclaim that when all judgment fell on Jesus the Old Testament standard exemplified by the law passed away. Has all judgment passed away in the New Testament? If God does not judge because of Christ's work on the cross, why does the ascended seated King of Kings still judge the churches in Revelations 2 and 3 by the standard of the law? Jesus' actions in Revelations 2 and 3 spoken to New Testament churches prove the fallacy of their teachings. In the New Testament if we walk in the Spirit, we fulfill the law.

Any teacher who says Jesus does not judge according to the law voids the whole book of Revelation. Diminishing the book of Revelation is not a wise move. The seventh commandment of the law states in Exodus 20:14, *"You shall not commit adultery."* That is the law. David committed adultery, repented, and God redeemed his sin, but the sword never departed from his family. The question is, Does Jesus judge according to the law today? In Revelation 2:20-22 speaking to the church at Thyatira the Lord says:

> *Nevertheless I have a few things against you, because you allow that woman Jezebel, who calls herself a prophetess, to teach and beguile My servants to commit sexual immorality and to eat things sacrificed to idols. And I gave her time to repent of her sexual immorality, and she did not repent. Indeed I will cast her into a sickbed, and those who commit* ***adultery with her*** *into great tribulation, unless they repent of their deeds.*

The question is, does the New Testament, resurrected, ascended Christ still judge according to the law? In addressing the church in Thyatira one would have to conclude that He absolutely does! This reveals the error of teachers who proclaim judicial principles of the Old Testament do not apply to us in the New. The Bible is the story of blood covenants and God has never broken one of them yet!

The first commandment in Exodus 20 is, *"You shall have no other gods before Me."* We are told in the book of Mark 12:30 that we, *"...shall love the Lord our God with all our heart, and...mind and... strength."* In Revelation 2:4-5 we are told, *"Nevertheless I have this against you, that you have left your first love. Remember therefore from where you have fallen; repent and do the first works, or else I will come to you quickly and remove your lampstand from its place – unless you repent."* It is obvious that judgments in Revelation still come based on the righteous standard of the law. Those who teach that there is no more judgment because Jesus died to take it all upon Himself, obviously have not read Revelation. Misguided ministers can help to nullify what Jesus came to fulfill. Biblical concepts, taught or applied ***out of context***, can nullify foundational biblical principles upon which the New Testament stands. The entire New Testament was formulated by revelation of the Old or divine encounter.

Did Jesus take judgment for sin on Himself? Yes! We are accepted in Christ. And His blood cleanses us when we fall. Jesus also suffered injustice. When ministers take away a revelation of Jesus the Judge, the church is at risk of losing all fear of the Lord. Jesus the Judge is about ready to re-emerge in the church and it is time we get to know Him for WHO HE IS! He is the same in the New Testament as in the Old Testament. Jesus judged Ananias and Sapphira, and He has judged minister friends of mine who would not repent. The fastest way to shorten your life is to begin believing Jesus no longer judges sin!

In Acts 12:1 Herod the king reached out to touch the church. He killed James and jailed Peter, intending to bring him out for the same fate. The church began to pray. They started to intercede. An angel was sent to release Peter from jail. But that was not the end of the story. In verses 21-23 we find that just as Herod reached out to touch the church, God reached out to touch Herod. We are told, *"So on a set day Herod, arrayed in royal apparel, sat on his throne and gave an oration to them. And the people kept shouting, 'The voice of a god and not a man!' Then immediately an angel of the Lord struck him because he did not give glory to God. And he was eaten by worms and died."* The church prayed and God touched Herod just as Herod touched the New Testament leadership. For those who question this principle of covenant justice, Revelation 16:4-6 should finish the debate:

> *Then the third angel poured out his bowl on the rivers and springs of water and they became blood. And I heard the angel of the waters saying: "You are righteous, O Lord, The One who is and who was and who is to be, Because You have judged these things. For they have shed the blood of saints and prophets, And You have given them blood to drink. For it is their* ***just due****."*

The Greek word for *"just due"* is **ax-ee-os** and is a weight and measure term. It simply means, 'the weight of another thing of like value.' *The Complete Word Study Dictionary of the New Testament* defines **ax-ee-os** as, 'Referring to a set of commercial balance scales, where the weights balance the beam determining cost, strictly bringing up the other beam of the scales.' It is used for those deserving either good or evil. It is obvious from the context that, just as God promised covenant justice to Abram ("*Those who bless you, I will bless. Those who curse you I will curse*"), covenant justice is still manifesting in the book of Revelation. There is no change. Justice is consistent!

Hebrews proclaims, *"Jesus Christ is the same yesterday, today and forever"* for the specific reason of guaranteeing covenant promises – there is no change. Why is it that we have so many people in the church who not only do not realize they have access to Throne-Room Justice but never ever ask for it! When the Israelites in Egypt cried out for justice, they were heard! Isn't it time for the persecuted church in the lands of Islam to cry out for justice? Isn't it time for the persecuted believers in Middle Eastern countries to cry out for justice? Where are the cries for justice from the church in Canada? Where are the cries for justice from the American church against judges who discount Godly righteous values? Covenant justice is alive and well. *"Jesus Christ is the same yesterday, today and forever,"* and His justice is just as accessible in the New Testament as it was in the Old. Why then do we have so few asking for that justice in a season where it is desperately needed and may well save the nation? It is time that the church began to rise up and restore biblical justice to the land! It is only a prayer away!

O Mighty Creator
And Covenant Keeper,
Author of justice & right,
Help us to stand tall
For perversion to fall,
Inviting Your truth and Your light

Jayne Houghton

Chapter 5

Kings and Priests

The fastest rising crime in the world today is identity theft. In America, one year renders upwards of ten million victims, costing five billion dollars annually and rising. The truth of the matter is there has been an identity theft that has gone on for several centuries and the church has yet to recover! We know from John 10:10 that *"The thief does not come except to steal, and to kill, and to destroy."* Perhaps his greatest tactic is that he has stolen the spiritual identity of the church. Revelation 1:4-6 states:

> *John, to the seven churches which are in Asia: Grace to you and peace from Him who is and who was and who is to come, and from the seven Spirits who are before His throne, and from Jesus Christ, the faithful witness, the firstborn from the dead, and the ruler over the kings of the earth. To Him who loved us and washed us from our sins in His own blood, and has made us* ***kings*** *and priests to His God and Father, to Him be glory and dominion forever and ever. Amen.*

Jesus bought and paid for rulership. His sacrifice made us Kings as well as Priests. He is the One with ultimate dominion, bought and paid for by three days and three nights in the belly of the earth where He forcibly removed all authority from the enemy upon His resurrection. Being a King is a very specific assignment that demands not only jurisdiction but also requires different levels of authority. From the Great Commission in Matthew 28:18-20 we know that jurisdiction is settled once and for all through this statement, *"Then Jesus came and spoke to them, saying, 'All authority has been given to Me in heaven and on earth. Go therefore and make disciples of all the nations, baptizing them in the name of the Father and of the Son and of the Holy Spirit, teaching them to observe all things that I have commanded you; and lo, I am with you always, even to the end of the age.' Amen."* The Great Commission settles the issue of jurisdiction. Anywhere we go on assignment from heaven, anywhere our foot treads, we carry as New Testament covenant believers ultimate jurisdiction from the Throne-Room! Let us settle it in our hearts!

Now the problem with having jurisdiction is that we also have to have corresponding authority to enforce law in that jurisdiction. We may have spiritual jurisdiction but if we are in a territory where the enemy has been granted authority *then* the conflict rages and jurisdiction alone will not necessarily win out. Paul addresses this issue in Ephesians 1:15-23 in a prayer for revelation of the different levels of authority that we might need to access in our assigned jurisdiction. This passage says:

> *Therefore I also, after I heard of your faith in the Lord Jesus and your love for all the saints, do not cease to give thanks for you, making mention of you in my prayers: that the God of our Lord Jesus Christ, the Father of glory, may give to you the spirit of wisdom and revelation in the knowledge of Him, the eyes of your understanding being enlightened; that you may know what is the hope of His calling, what are the riches of the glory of His inheritance in the saints, and what is*

> *the exceeding greatness of His power toward us who believe, according to the working of His mighty power which He worked in Christ when He raised Him from the dead and seated Him at His right hand in the heavenly places, far above all principality and power and might and dominion, and every name that is named, not only in this age but also in that which is to come. And He put all things under His feet, and gave Him to be head over all things to the church, which is His body, the fullness of Him who fills all in all.*

Without a revelation of the authority to match an assigned jurisdiction, then we are in trouble. In a season of restoration we can expect the full measure of God-given authority at every level to be restored in order for the end-time harvest to be procured. The real question at the initial phase of this restoration is how did we lose this Kingly authority? The answer very simply is that the Priestly ministry was over-emphasized. Receiving mercy for salvation qualifies us to extend it to others. Our experience becomes the qualification. Jesus made us Kings but where do we go for the experience? The five-fold ministry of Ephesians 4:11 have the responsibility of building this into the church for the last days!

1 Samuel 8:4-5 reveals the job of a king. We are told, *"Then all the elders of Israel gathered together and came to Samuel at Ramah, and said to him, 'Look, you are old, and your sons do not walk in your ways. Now make for us a king to judge us like all the nations.'"* The primary job of a King was to judge the people. Priests brought salvation. Kings brought justice! The church through lack of knowledge has forfeited its Kingly call. When we do not know we cannot do! Faith comes by hearing God's Word. Our teaching has emphasized Priestly ministry and consequently diminished Kingly authority.

In 1 Kings 3 Solomon is presented with the problem of two women,

both claiming one living son. Each woman had a son but one died in the night. The woman whose son died placed her dead son in the arms of the other while she slept and took that woman's living son. Solomon heard the claim and counterclaim and proclaimed in 1 Kings 3:23-27:

> *...The one says, "This is my son, who lives, and your son is the dead one"; and the other says, "No! But your son is the dead one, and my son is the living one." Then the king said, "Bring me a sword." So they brought a sword before the king. And the king said, "Divide the living child in two, and give half to one, and half to the other." Then the woman whose son was living spoke to the king, for she yearned with compassion for her son; and she said, "O my lord, give her the living child, and by no means kill him! But the other said, "Let him be neither mine nor yours, but divide him." So the king answered and said, "Give the first woman the living child, and by no means kill him; she is his mother."*

What is interesting about this passage is how Israel responded to Solomon's unusual display of divine wisdom. Verse 28 declares, *"And all Israel heard of the judgment which the king had rendered; and they feared the king, for they saw that the wisdom of God was in him to administer justice."*

The job of a King is to administer the justice of God! The job of a Priest is to bring salvation to people. Most of us have spent our lives developing the Priestly side of ministry and have paid little or no attention to the Kingly side. By emphasizing Matthew 7, *"Judge not, that you be not judged,"* without setting it in context, we have eroded the foundation of the Kingly ministry. If we had been present to hear Jesus we could have caught the cadence of His message which completely changes the application of *"Judge not, that you be not judged."*

The cadence of Jesus' message begins in Matthew 6:1 where He says "give," but do not give like the hypocrites. In verse 5 He says "pray," but do not pray like the hypocrites. In verse 16 it is "fast," but do not fast like the hypocrites. By the time we get to Matthew 7:1, we would have understood *"judge"* in the same cadence, '...but do not judge like the hypocrites.' Kings have the primary assignment of asserting God's dominion by judging because their job is to bring the justice of God into every situation where injustice rises. We have equipped the church to be Priests who capably minister salvation but we have failed in preparing the church to bring forth the justice of God. As injustice rises the Kingly assignment grows in importance. There are pockets of people who can never be reached with a Priestly message until a Kingly judicial manifestation opens the door. The Apostle Paul found himself in just such a place in Acts 13 when he faced a false prophet. Kings administer justice. Priests administer salvation. We are called to do both.

The first thing we need to realize about the Lord Jesus is that He was both Priest and King and His Priestly ministry is seen in the gospels while His Kingly ministry is seen after the resurrection. In Matthew 10:8 Jesus is very Priestly. He says, *"Heal the sick, cleanse the lepers, raise the dead, cast out demons. Freely you have received, freely give."* Jesus imparts an anointing, lights the candlestick of the Twelve, and sends them off to minister in the power of the Holy Spirit. But in Revelation chapter 2:4-5, He says to the church of Ephesus, *"Nevertheless I have this against you, that you have left your first love. Remember therefore from where you have fallen; repent and do the first works, or else I will come to you quickly and remove your lampstand from its place – unless you repent."* In the gospels Jesus lit their candlestick as a Priest. In Revelation 2 to the church of Ephesus He said, "If you don't repent, I will remove your candlestick." Removing the candlestick is the prerogative of a King!

In John chapter 8:1-11 Jesus ministers to a woman who is caught in adultery. He is very, very Priestly. He says, *"Neither do I condemn you; go and sin no more."* But in Revelation chapter 2:20-22, addressing the church at Thyatira, Jesus says this, *"Nevertheless I have a few things against you, because you allow that woman Jezebel, who calls herself a prophetess, to teach and beguile My servants to commit sexual immorality and to eat things sacrificed to idols. And I gave her time to repent of her sexual immorality, and she did not repent. Indeed I will cast her into a sickbed, and those who commit adultery with her into great tribulation, unless they repent of their deeds."*

In the gospels, as a Priest, Jesus forgives the woman caught in adultery. In Revelation 2, as the Judge of all the earth, He commands those in the church of Thyatira to repent or else they are going to be thrown into great tribulation. Once Jesus ascended, He became the Judge of all the earth starting with the church. We cannot faithfully represent Jesus the Judge if we only know Jesus the Savior.

In 1 Peter 2:18-24 we are told:

> *Servants, be submissive to your masters with all fear, not only to the good and gentle, but also to the harsh. For this is commendable, if because of conscience toward God one endures grief, suffering wrongfully. For what credit is it if, when you are beaten for your faults, you take it patiently? But when you do good and suffer for it, if you take it patiently, this is commendable before God. For to this you were called, because Christ also suffered for us, leaving us an example, that you should follow His steps: "Who committed no sin, Nor was guile found in His mouth," who, when He was reviled, did not revile in return; when he suffered, He did not threaten, but committed Himself to Him*

who judges righteously; who Himself bore our sins in His own body on the tree, that we, having died to sins, might live for righteousness – by whose stripes you were healed.

While Peter is very, very Priestly and warns us that when we are reviled not to revile in return and when we suffer not to threaten but to commit ourselves to Him who judges righteously, in Acts 5:1-3 he transitions very quickly into Kingly mode and announces the death of Ananias and Sapphira. They fall at his feet – dead! How is it that he can exhort us to be Priestly and then in Acts 5 transition into another man acting like the Judge of all the earth in declaring the death of Ananias and Sapphira? When facing insidious sin threatening the young church, Peter brought Throne-Room justice! The judgment seat of Christ was manifested at Peter's feet!

Those of us in ministry are responsible for the condition of the church. By emphasizing Jesus the Savior, we have hidden Jesus the Judge. Jesus the Judge delivered the early church from mammon by removing the carriers. As ministers we have prepared the church to attempt to save the carriers instead of by faith removing them. Jesus in Revelation kills in order to save. Do we know Him? Month after month and year after year we continue to lose our nation generation after generation. Freedoms our forefathers died for are now gone. The unsanctified mercy we prayed has enabled renegade judges to continue sitting on the bench and stealing our heritage. There is little fear of God in the church and none in the government! That will only change when the church represents Jesus the Judge. God consistently saved by removing the enemy in answer to prayer. We have covenant access to a Judicial Throne. Let's learn to use it!

The Apostle Paul had to follow in the same footsteps as Peter in learning about the two ministries of the Lord Jesus. In Romans 12, Paul exhorts us in verses 17-21 to be very Priestly:

> *Repay no one evil for evil. Have regard for good things in the sight of all men. If it is possible, as much as depends on you, live peaceably with all men. Beloved, do not avenge yourselves, but rather give place to wrath; for it is written, "Vengeance is Mine, I will repay," says the Lord. "Therefore if your enemy hungers, feed him; If he thirsts, give him a drink; For in so doing you will heap coals of fire on his head." Do not be overcome by evil, but overcome evil with good.*

Immediately in Romans 13:1-4 Paul declares the Kingly judicial side of Christ:

> *Let every soul be subject to the governing authorities. For there is no authority except from God, and the authorities that exist are appointed by God. Therefore whoever resists the authority resists the ordinance of God, and those who resist will bring judgment on themselves. For rulers are not a terror to good works, but to evil. Do you want to be unafraid of the authority? Do what is good, and you will have praise from the same. For he is God's minister to you for good. But if you do evil, be afraid; for he does not bear the sword in vain; for he is God's minister, an avenger to execute wrath on him who practices evil.*

Paul ends Romans 12 with an exhortation to be Priestly as a witness for salvation and then immediately contrasts the Priestly ministry with the Kingly. Government is a function of the Kingly anointing and carries the authority to execute covenant judgment on those who practice evil. Jesus bought and paid for authority as a Priest and King.

The unique thing about this application is to look at how in Romans 12 Paul tells us that if our enemy is thirsty, give him a drink but in Acts

13, when he faces a formidable enemy who through deception is keeping him out of an assigned territory, he does not give him a drink. Acts 13:9-11 says:

> *Then Saul, who also is called Paul, filled with the Holy Spirit, looked intently at him and said, "O full of all deceit and all fraud, you son of the devil, you enemy of all righteousness, will you not cease perverting the straight ways of the Lord? And now, indeed, the hand of the Lord is upon you, and you shall be blind, not seeing the sun for a time." And immediately a dark mist fell on him, and he went around seeking someone to lead him by the hand.*

Paul did not have any hesitation in tapping the Kingly anointing when it was needed in order to break through a barrier. The Kingly anointing enabled him to bring a Priestly message. In the American church we know the Jesus of the gospels but we do not know the Jesus of Revelation. Paul got to know Him well enough to represent Him. Why don't we know the Jesus of Revelation? Have we abandoned learning the principles of justice? From Genesis to Revelation the laws governing justice are consistent. Jesus was resurrected and ascended, and when He took a seat at the right hand of God He became THE KING, THE JUDGE OF ALL THE EARTH and He exhorts us to learn how to be agents of justice. As an agent of justice we have a responsibility. The question is, are we going to accept it and pay the price to grow into the ability to enforce it?

Matthew 5:13 perfectly describes a church culture which focuses on the Priestly ministry of salvation but is completely lost, ignorant, or unaware of its Kingly authority. Jesus said, *"You are the salt of the earth, but if the salt loses its flavor, how shall it be seasoned? It is then **good for nothing** but to be thrown out and trampled underfoot by men."* The word *"good"* is the Greek word **is-khoo-o** and **is-khoo-o** is a word whose usage establishes divine justice. The best dictionary for the Bible is the Bible. Accurate interpretation demands we let the Bible define itself. **Is-khoo-o** is used in James chapter 5 concerning the ability of a believer to move God's Hand. James 5:16-18 says:

> *Confess your trespasses to one another, and pray for one another, that you may be healed. The effective, fervent prayer of a righteous man avails much (**is-khoo-o**). Elijah was a man with a nature like ours, and he prayed earnestly that it would not rain; and it did not rain on the land for three years and six months. And he prayed again, and the heaven gave rain, and the earth produced its fruit.*

James tells us that in covenant there is no difference between us and Elijah. Jesus said that John the Baptist was the greatest prophet in the Old Testament but, 'He who is least in the [N.T.] kingdom is greater than John the Baptist.' *"The effective, fervent prayer of a righteous man..."* brings **is-khoo-o** on the scene and the example is bringing judgment on a national scale by closing down an agrarian economy. Crippling the agrarian economy through drought brought a showdown with the prophets of Baal to save the land. Wicked king Ahab forfeited the anointing to bring justice by his sinful choices, and God released it to Elijah instead.

King Ahab believed Elijah's judicial authority crippled the economy of the nation. 1 Kings 18:17-18 states, *"Then it happened, when Ahab saw Elijah, that Ahab said to him, 'Is that you, O troubler of Israel?' And he answered, 'I have not troubled Israel, but you and your father's house have, in that you have forsaken the commandments of the LORD, and you have followed the Baals'."* When we allow the Bible to define itself, it presents a yardstick by which we can answer whether or not we have salt. If we can move God's Hand in justice to stop the modern day Ahabs and Jezebels then we have salt. From the time we were saved, we have been taught to bless people and pray for our enemies – that is Priestly. Jesus challenges us to have salt like Elijah who prayed against the economy and devastated it to remove the defiling proponents of Baal. Democrats and Republicans who support abortion and homosexual marriage are exactly like the prophets of Baal. Ahab is represented by every minister who by choice refuses to confront sin to gain a larger audience and greater success. One example of Jezebel is every national and local media outlet championing political correctness. Another manifestation of Jezebel is seen with the spreading of poison in the majority of university classes where she owns the pulpit. Let the salt arise! Any denomination which chooses to ordain homosexuals or bless homosexual unions should be baptized in salt until they share the same fate as Ahab and the prophets of Baal they promote.

1 Kings 17:1-7 outlines the beginning of this process,

> *And Elijah the Tishbite, of the inhabitants of Gilead, said to Ahab, "As the LORD God of Israel lives, before whom I stand, there shall not be dew nor rain these years, except at my word." Then the word of the LORD came to him, saying, "Get away from here and turn eastward, and hide by the Brook Cherith, which flows into the Jordan. And it will be that you shall drink from the brook, and I have commanded the ravens to feed you there." So he went and did according to the word of the LORD, for he went and stayed by the Brook Cherith, which flows into the Jordan. The ravens brought him bread and meat in the morning, and bread and meat in the evening; and he drank from the brook. And it happened after a while that the brook dried up, because there had been no rain in the land.*

The first thing we need to realize in this process is that Elijah prayed specifically to stop all rain therefore devastating the agrarian economy of the day. Three and one-half years of no rain would cripple any economy and bring a nation to its knees. The purpose was justice/judgment for the prophets of Baal. God released an anointing to bring devastation, death and destruction. The perpetrators of the defilement, the king and his family were diligently looking to apprehend Elijah to kill him. God was willing to reduce the economy to nothing in order to confront what was defiling the nation.

The Kingly anointing brings justice and in this case gave the people a choice as to who they were going to serve.

1 Kings 18:37-40 states:

> *"Hear me, O LORD, hear me, that this people may know that You are the LORD God, and that You have turned their hearts back to You again." Then the fire of the LORD fell and consumed the burnt sacrifice, and the wood and the stones and the dust, and it licked up the water that was in the trench. Now when all the people saw it, they fell on their faces; and they said, "The LORD, He is God! The LORD, He is God!" And Elijah said to them, "Seize the prophets of Baal! Do not let one of them escape!" So they seized them; and Elijah brought them down to the Brook Kishon and executed them there.*

God initiated this judgment through Elijah. God saved the nation by judging. Having salt means bringing justice. The fire fell and the prophets of Baal were executed! The same spirit that inspired Ahab and Jezebel is resident in nations and manifested in some preachers and politicians. Jesus exhorted every believer to have salt! If we do not have a relationship with God that can bring a Kingly judicial anointing then we have lost our salt. Salt represents our ability to preserve a society from a course of utter destruction. When there are voices in a culture that parallel the perversion of Ahab and Jezebel by demanding that a nation support that which the Bible forbids – salt is needed! How would Elijah have prayed for Supreme Court Justices who in their individual arrogance are attempting to legislate Sodom and Gomorrah? We have salt when we can pray the Hand of God on those errant justices and see them removed from office. According to Jesus, anything less in the New Testament simply means we have lost our salt! Our traditions have blinded us to the judicial ministry of Christ. Jesus is seeking a people who will judge and war with Him. Will we answer the call? Are we ready to regain our salt? If so, we can in faith pray against those whose intent is establishing evil!

The church does a good job ministering mercy and salvation to the individual, but stops there. The covenant makes salt available to benefit the nation. Applying salt on a national level means entering the Kingly realm. Elijah was willing to pay the price to enter this realm – are we? The Holy Spirit interrupted one of my complaining sessions about government by stating, "Don't complain if you haven't used your authority and prayed against the evil!" Christians are so full of mercy that often we have to be forced into action by adversity. Judy Ross, a member of the Betsy Ross family who created the American Flag, states about her grandfather:

> *My grandfather was a pioneer minister in the early 1900s. He was saved and filled with the Spirit as a result of the Azusa outpouring. This incident I'm about to share took place sometime in the mid 1920s in Arkansas where he had started one of many churches. The Pentecostal churches were typically on the wrong side of the tracks. With little else for entertainment three young men showed up at my grandfather's church. One was the son of the town judge, the other the son of the*

town doctor and the third the son of the local sheriff. They amused themselves throughout the service by mocking and ridiculing what was taking place. Elders of the church had gone to them and asked them to be quiet or leave, with no result. My Irish grandfather took all that he was going to take. In the middle of his sermon he turned to them pointed his finger and said, "I turn you over into the hands of the living God." They were immediately struck blind. [Notice that he did not turn them over to satan – They were unbelievers and already in his pocket.] This, of course, terminated the service except for the two that repented. The one who was still blind was led home by the other two imploring him to repent. He did not.

Why wait until we have to be forced into action? Prepare now by learning your covenant. If we learn about justice like we learned about the gifts of the Spirit, faith will rise and action will follow. We are called to be agents of justice!

When will the evil change? The answer: when we decide to pick up the salt and pray against those legislating it. The Lord is ready and waiting on us.

Jesus gave the disciples an unforgettable example as He taught about this Kingly anointing when He cleansed the temple. This event was so offensive it resulted in His crucifixion. In Mark 11:11,12 we are told, *"And Jesus went into Jerusalem and into the temple. So when He had looked around at all things, as the hour was already late, He went out to Bethany with the twelve."* Jesus went in, surveyed the temple, saw the mismanagement, saw the rulership of the spirit of mammon, saw the entire religious system captive to a defiling abominable spirit. Jesus formulated a plan and executed it! On the next day, verses 13-14 state, *"And seeing from afar a fig tree having leaves, He went to see if perhaps He would find something on it. And when He came to it, He found nothing but leaves, for it was not the season for figs. In response Jesus said to it, 'Let no one eat fruit from you ever again.' And His disciples heard it."* On the way into the temple He saw a fig tree, which was exactly like the leadership of the temple – leafy green, looked great but produced no eternal fruit. He spoke death to the tree. We know He cursed it because Peter comments about it in verses 20-21, *"Now in the morning, as they passed by, they saw the fig tree dried up from the roots. And Peter, remembering, said to Him, 'Rabbi, look! The fig tree which You cursed has withered away.'"* The very next day the fig tree was dead.

Peter noticed the dead fig tree after Jesus cleansed the temple in verses 15-19. Jesus used this example to teach and declare what faith in God would accomplish whether cleansing a temple or in Elijah's case cleansing a nation. Verses 22-24 of Mark 11 state:

> *So Jesus answered and said to them, "Have faith in God. For assuredly, I say to you, whoever says to this mountain, 'Be removed and be cast into the sea,' and does not doubt in his heart, but believes that those things he says will come to pass, he will have whatever he says. Therefore I say to you, whatever things you ask when you pray, believe that you receive them, and you will have them."*

We know that Jesus had judicial authority in mind here because when we look at the parallel passage in Matthew 21:21-22 the initial emphasis is on killing the fig tree, *"So Jesus answered and said to them, 'Assuredly, I say to you, if you have faith and do not doubt, you will not only do what was done to the fig tree, but also if you say to this mountain, "Be removed and be cast into the sea," it will be done. And all things, whatever you ask in prayer, believing, you will receive.'"* The very first thing mentioned in Matthew's account is not removing the mountain. The first thing Matthew keys in on is killing fig trees. Jesus understood Kingly authority. He understood the church had to move in it. He also understood it was a choice. Our political landscape is full of leafy green fruitless fig trees. Why have we removed no fig trees? Is our Priestly tradition so strong that we fail to represent the Kingly when we are led? Jesus both modeled and taught judicial imprecatory prayer. How could we have neglected His teaching for so many years? Jesus released justice through His words. Death and life are in the power of the tongue. When He spoke death to the fig tree, it died. God authored and honored His words. The difference between Eli and Samuel was God honored Samuel's words. Eli allowed mammon and sexual immorality while Samuel did not. Live like Samuel so that God will honor your words.

Where is the church when it comes to the issue of justice? The answer is seemingly saltless. Is there a path out of saltlessness? Absolutely! We must run and not walk out of saltlessness!

Every Christian should be an agent of God's justice and if we are not we will stand before the judgment seat of Christ and give an account for why we spent the majority of our spiritual life saltless. Blaming saltlessness on ministers while spiritually probable may not absolve the majority of us from personal guilt!

Jesus was very explicit with the Twelve about the necessity of maintaining their salt. In Mark 9:49-50 He said, *"For everyone will be seasoned with fire, and every sacrifice will be seasoned with salt. Salt is good, but if the salt loses its flavor, how will you season it? Have salt in yourselves, and have peace with one another."* The issue of a priest salting the sacrifice goes to the very core of the Priestly ministry. A priest without the ability to salt a sacrifice cannot consummate the covenant – he cannot fully do his job. What biblical issues forfeit salt? Perhaps the number one issue is money or a spirit of mammon. But that is so broad, wide, and deep it is the subject of a book all its own entitled *Purifying the Altar.* **WARNING: Do not even consider attempting to exercise the Kingly anointing if you are associated with an impure altar – personal or corporate. Because the altar sanctifies the gift, you must not be associated with impure altars by sowing into them. If you associate with an impure altar you will not be able to stand in the fire you have to kindle as a King. To execute a Kingly anointing, you must be able to stand in the fire you call down! Eli could not and Samuel could. Therefore be like Samuel!**

Peter understood the purity necessary to successfully confront Ananias and Sapphira. He identified defiling contributors in 2 Peter 2:14, *"...having eyes full of adultery and that cannot cease from sin, beguiling unstable souls. They have a heart trained in covetous practices, and are accursed children."* An impure altar is one where covetous practices prevail.

The top three Charismatic covetous practices that make an altar impure and therefore dangerous for contributions are: (1)"The Lord told me there are 20 people here who are going to give a thousand dollars!" In the Didache the apostles warned churches about false prophets stating, "And no prophet when he ordereth a table in the spirit, shall eat of it." Prophesying something we benefit from makes us a false prophet and guarantees that what is placed on the altar is defiled rather than sanctified and completed. 2 Peter 2:18 warns of *"...For when they speak great swelling words of emptiness, they allure through the lusts of the flesh, through licentiousness, the ones who have actually escaped from those who live in error"* which applies to (2) hyping signs, wonders and miracles for drawing a crowd and improving offerings. This is equally abominable as feigning the word of knowledge and saddles all those who sow into it with the dysfunction of the originator. God intended ministry to establish a pure altar where covenantal giving could be rewarded. Spiritually we become one with the altar we sow into! (3) In Acts 20 Paul told the Ephesian elders he was innocent of their blood because he had not diminished the whole counsel of God. Many leaders choose a ministry model which excludes scripture that confronts sin. When this compromising spirit weaves its way through an altar the impact can be doubly devastating. I consistently hear the same phrase from those who attend such churches. "I'm so hungry." When eating half rations a person inevitably gets very hungry but has to fight off compromise to get to the truth! Let us flee impure altars so we can gain our full quotient of salt! Enhance our discernment and overcome deception by studying *Purifying the Altar.* We cannot dispense justice if we are joined to an impure altar!

Jesus made us Kings and Priests for a reason. The Kingly anointing can only manifest through a Priestly heart where diligence and maturity are displayed to maintain salt. How do we maintain salt? The answer is in Mark 9. Verses 33-37 identify the chief issue the Twelve were struggling with at the time,

> *Then He came to Capernaum. And when He was in the house He asked them, "What was it you disputed among yourselves on the road?" But they kept silent, for on the road they had disputed among themselves who would be the greatest. And He sat down, called the twelve, and said to them, "If anyone desires to be first, he shall be last of all and servant of all." Then He took a little child and set him in the midst of them. And when He had taken him in His arms, He said to them, "Whoever receives one of these little children in My name receives Me; and whoever receives Me, receives not Me but Him who sent Me."*

Selfish ambition was rampant among the Twelve and they were all vying for position. The top position had another benefit – control over the treasury. Apparently the teaching on servanthood had gone in one ear and out the other.

John, the favorite, displayed a judicial choice but it was outside of a properly exercised Priestly heart. Jesus had to correct it. Verses 38-41 state:

> *Now John answered Him, saying, "Teacher, we saw someone who does not follow us casting out demons in Your name, and we forbade him because he does not follow us." But Jesus said, "Do not forbid him, for no one who works a miracle in My name can soon afterward speak evil of Me. For he who is not against us is on our side. For whoever gives you a cup of water to drink in My name, because you belong to Christ, assuredly, I say to you, he will by no means lose his reward."*

Just because an individual was not part of the Twelve they assumed he did not have the right to move in the anointing. Jesus corrected them on that quickly!

He went on to declare principles that should cause everyone to tremble. Jesus said in verses 42-43, *"And whoever causes one of these little ones who believe in Me to stumble, it would be better for him if a millstone were hung around his neck, and he were thrown into the sea. And if your hand makes you sin, cut it off. It is better for you to enter into life maimed, than having two hands, to go to hell, into the fire that shall never be quenched."* Jesus demanded drastic action against attitudes which were fleshly and which defiled a person to the point of losing their salt. There is no way to operate in a Kingly anointing from a position of strife or selfish ambition. Jesus made it dramatically clear to the Twelve and consequently to us in Mark 9:44-48 that this is an issue about which we must be specifically serious:

Where "their worm does not die and the fire is not quenched." And if your foot makes you sin, cut it off. It is better for you to enter life lame, than having two feet, to be cast into hell, into the fire that shall never be quenched – where "their worm does not die and the fire is not quenched." And if your eye makes you sin, pluck it out. It is better for you to enter the kingdom of God with one eye, than having two eyes, to be cast into hell fire – where "their worm does not die and the fire is not quenched."'

To stand before Jesus and hear, *"Well done, good and faithful servant,"* demands that we deal with the same fleshly motivations as the Twelve and come to a place of servanthood where the chief issue is the will of the Spirit, not our own personal ambitions.

The Twelve, for three and a half years, enjoyed face-to-face relationship with the Creator only to culminate in seeming dramatic failure. Perhaps their failure in denying Christ was the greatest preparation for serving Him in the New Testament church. They discovered through failure the necessity of relying on the power of the Holy Spirit because the ability to do it was not in them. Paul dramatically outlines this struggle between the flesh and the spirit in Romans. Jesus demanded that we have salt in ourselves. Having salt in ourselves, means the ability to simultaneously move in both a Priestly and Kingly anointing. Two passages that spell this out are referred to in the Sermon on the Mount and the James 5 alert about Elijah's prayer of faith. Justice is available from the Throne-Room and until the church manifests it they are showing a distinct lack of salt.

Justice for a Priest and justice for a King have very different manifestations. Justice for a Priest means that salvation flows where God's people are empowered to reach the fullness of their destiny. They are encouraged, blessed, and failures are redeemed along the way. We seem to have a natural propensity to go in this direction because it is very redemptive. It is based on mercy that forgives sin. Justice for a King does not forgive sin, it punishes sin with judgment and therefore cleanses the land. It is an entirely different mindset. The problem with the church today is that we view justice only through the corrective eyeglasses of a Priest. It is catastrophic to refuse to view justice through the eyes of a biblical King, thereby never embracing the King's anointing that is offered to every believer. In Christianity our sense of Priestly justice comes from the gospels. God sacrificed His Son to forgive us – we have mercy for everyone. But once Jesus was resurrected, once He ascended, once He took a seat at the right Hand of God, He entered a distinct and different ministry. He entered the ministry of a King. We are told in Revelation 19:11 exactly what He looks like as that King, *"Then I saw heaven opened, and behold, a white horse. And He who sat on him was called Faithful and True, and in righteousness He judges and makes war."* Jesus in Revelation has always been ready to judge and war in behalf of the church. Previous generations found Him. We must if we are to gain the Priestly harvest promised. Our eyes have been blinded to Jesus the Judge. The Priestly message is much more profitable in building a successful ministry. We are stuck in a Priestly mindset and have never transitioned to sit with Jesus on the Throne and interact with the King of Kings and Lord of Lords who is ready to do for us what He did for David.

Justice for a Priest meant salvation. Justice for a King meant judgment. When Peter stood with Jesus in Acts 5 and proclaimed the death of Ananias and Sapphira, he manifested the justice of a King. Where is that mindset in the church today? Answer: It hardly even exists. It must be developed. It must be restored. And faith comes by hearing and hearing by the Word of God.

Will you shine
As I assign?
Will you declare
Hard words in prayer?

Jayne Houghton

Chapter 6

The Key of David

Revelation 1:6 says Jesus has made us *"...kings and priests to His God and Father, to Him be glory and dominion forever and ever. Amen."* Verses 17-18 say, *"And when I saw Him, I fell at His feet as dead. But he laid His right hand on me, saying to me, 'Do not be afraid; I am the First and the Last. I am He who lives, and was dead, and behold, I am alive forevermore. Amen. And I have the keys of Hades and of Death.'"* In the gospels Jesus offered keys to all who have a revelation of Christ. Matthew 16:18-19 states, *"And I also say to you that you are Peter, and on this rock I will build My church, and the gates of Hades shall not prevail against it. And I will give you the keys of the kingdom of heaven, and whatever you bind on earth will be bound in heaven, and whatever you loose on earth will be loosed in heaven."* Have we been taught primarily to use the keys for individual salvation? If so, then the keys for corporate salvation have taken a back seat to the point we do not think like David! Have we been taught to use the keys for justice?

We have keys that we have not used! There is no problem with Priestly justice. That means mercy for the sinner that results in salvation. But to every Israelite, Kingly justice had the reward of salvation in it – salvation derived from the King's office. His purpose was to judge and make war. In war the King brought salvation from those who were intent on destroying their nation. We have people today under the influence of spirits intent on destroying a harvest from the land. We have whole nations intent on destroying America and Israel. Romans 11 promises the church the nation of Israel as a harvest field. If we are to gain the Priestly justice of the harvest, it is becoming more and more apparent that we must recover the keys to Kingly justice and move in them as quickly as possible. Any national leader who promises to destroy a future harvest such as Israel should meet a Mordecai Ham prayer – God save him or kill him now! If he refuses to repent, call the ambulance!

To the church of Philadelphia, Jesus said, *"And to the angel of the church in Philadelphia write, 'These things says He who is holy, He who is true, "He who has the key of David, He who opens and no one shuts, and shuts and no one opens"* (Revelation 3:7). The keys of the Kingdom open and close doors of salvation or doors of judgment. This is why the covenant of "Sure Mercy" becomes a foundation for every application of Kingly justice. To become firmly established in this foundation, study our book *The Sure Mercies of David* because its content provides the substance of faith for justice!

It is essential to leave Jesus' words to the church at Philadelphia in the context of His interactions with the other churches. His initial words are very Priestly in verses 7-8, *"And to the angel of the church in Philadelphia write, 'These things says He who is holy, He who is true, "He who has the key of David, He who opens and no one shuts, and shuts and no one opens": I know your works, See, I have set before you an open door, and no one can shut it; for you have a little strength, have kept My word, and have not denied My name.'"* Are His words to five other churches more Kingly, Priestly, or a combination of both? Are these keys to be used as Kingly, Priestly, or both? How does Jesus use them in interacting with the other churches?

The first church that Jesus speaks to is the church at Ephesus. Jesus has good things to say about the church at Ephesus and commends them but He also has one area of correction. Revelation 2:4,5 states, *"Nevertheless I have this against you, that you have left your first love. Remember therefore from where you have fallen; repent and do the first works, or else I will come to you quickly and remove your lampstand from its place – unless you repent."* Jesus' initial use of the keys at Ephesus is judicial very much like Elijah's prayer for three and one-half years. One stopped the rain and the other threatened to stop all anointing. Jesus promised to use the key of David to shut off their anointing if they did not repent. If they refused to return to their first love and do their first works, then the anointing for their lampstand would be taken away. Jesus' first use of the key of David at Ephesus was judicial. Jesus' promise to use the key of David guaranteed that the ministry lampstand would completely dry up if there was no repentance. The key of David is available but how are we using it? Jesus died to put this key in our hand! Use it!

The next church is Smyrna where Jesus outlines a coming persecution and martyrdom. Jesus warns them about what is coming and commands them to be faithful unto death and they will gain the crown of life. That was probably not a welcomed message for the people of Smyrna – but it came as it is coming today to many Christians in Islamic nations. If Islam rules a nation, it is likely the Christians there have a lot in common with those in Smyrna.

Isaiah 9:6-7 states:

> *For unto us a Child is born, Unto us a Son is given; And the government will be upon His shoulder. And His name will be called Wonderful, Counselor, Mighty God, Everlasting Father, Prince of Peace. Of the increase of His government and peace There will be no end, Upon the throne of David and over His kingdom, To order it and establish it with judgment and justice From that time forward, even forever. The zeal of*

the LORD of hosts will perform this.

Isaiah chapter 9 gives us the foundation for the key of David of which Jesus speaks. The key of David is obvious in this passage. It is the anointing to order and establish the Kingdom with **mish-pawt** justice or judgment and **tsed-aw-kaw** which is righteousness based on the ethical or moral standard of God's Word. Isaiah 22:20-22 further amplifies this issue by stating, *"Then it shall be in that day, That I will call My servant Eliakim the son of Hilkiah; I will clothe him with your robe And strengthen him with your belt; I will commit your responsibility into his hand. He shall be a father to the inhabitants of Jerusalem And to the house of Judah. The key of the house of David I will lay on his shoulder; So he shall open, and no one shall shut; And he shall shut, and no one shall open."* The issue here is a governmental anointing that establishes the Kingdom through judgment and righteousness. When Jesus said in the New Testament, *"I will give you the keys of the kingdom"* He was speaking about the anointing of a King to establish justice – governmental Throne-Room justice bought and paid for through His own death, burial, and resurrection. Jesus confirmed the Davidic covenant of "Sure Mercy."

When Jesus spoke to the church at Pergamos He commended them for holding fast to His name, but then He identified an issue in which they were tolerating sin in their midst and the doctrine of the Nicolaitans which was dangerous. In Revelations 2, verse 16, Jesus talks like the Judge of all the earth when He says, *"Repent, or else I will come to you quickly and will fight against them with the sword of My mouth."* The keys of the kingdom deal with justice and judgment from a platform of righteousness. They are released by the God-breathed words we pray and the prophetic declarations we make.

Jesus compliments the church at Thyatira for their works and their increase, but if the increase is because of tolerating sin then they are on a destructive path. The politically correct choice to tolerate Jezebel and sexual immorality brought Jesus the Judge. Jesus commanded them to repent or they would find themselves thrown into a sickbed with great tribulation. Did Jesus tolerate seeker-sensitivity here?

Finally the last church preceding Philadelphia was the church at Sardis where Jesus commanded them to strengthen the things that remain. They had not finished the works they were called to do. They were commanded to hold fast and repent or He would come upon them as a thief executing justice/judgment.

When Jesus told the church of Philadelphia that He had the key of David that could open and no one could shut and shut and no one could open, He was dealing with the anointing for justice and judgment. It is available. It not only comes upon churches but it is available to the church for accomplishing assignments. This key should be used to close down the counterfeits among us. Peter used it. Paul used it. The end-time church is promised a double of what the early church possessed. The time is at hand!

In Hebrews 1:6-9 we are given the New Testament law of the extended scepter which says:

> *But when He again brings the first born into the world, He says: "Let all the angels of God worship Him." And of the angels He says: "Who makes His angels spirits And His ministers a flame of fire." But to the Son He says: "Your throne, O God, is forever and ever; A scepter of righteousness is the scepter of Your Kingdom. You have loved righteousness and hated lawelessness; Therefore God, Your God, has anointed You With the oil of gladness more than Your companions."*

In the days of Mordecai and Esther, when Esther was weighing the price of helping save the Jewish nation, her chief issue was whether or not the king would extend the scepter once she went in to him without being summoned, which was the law of kings in those days.

One of the great blessings of the New Covenant is that every believer who qualifies has an open extended scepter at all times, to enter the Throne-Room of the Creator of the heavens and the earth. There are two qualifications: (1) Receive Jesus as Savior and accept His blood for the forgiveness of all sin. (2) Choose to walk in and maintain righteousness according to God's moral standard. The scepter that is extended to us is a scepter of righteousness, so the open scepter demands that we walk in the Spirit and not fulfill the desires of the flesh and maintain righteousness through the blood. For all those who choose to walk that way, they have an extended scepter guaranteeing them a hearing in the Throne-Room, and they can access not only salvation as a Priest but justice as a King. Where are the Christian Kings and where is the justice of the Lord for which Jesus died? The five-fold ministry has fallen short when we have hardly anyone walking in the fullness of Christ. The whole purpose of team ministry is to bring the church into the fullness of Christ. When the church is equipped to minister Priestly salvation but is unaware of Kingly governmental justice, then the five-fold ministry has failed its assignment. Until the church can stand up and move the Hand of God, as Paul did in Acts 13, we have failed to prepare a generation to wind up the age.

The scepter of righteousness is extended – we must become comfortable with the Kingly call!

In Matthew 28 Jesus gave the Great Commission sending us out to *"...make disciples of all the nations."* In Matthew 24 the disciples had asked Him what would be the sign of His coming and the end of the age. His answer in verses 7-14 can at times be difficult to hear:

> *For nation will rise against nation, and kingdom against kingdom. And there will be famines, pestilences, and earthquakes in various places. All these are the beginning of sorrows. Then they will deliver you up to tribulation and kill you, and you will be hated by all nations for My name's sake. And then many will be offended, will betray one another, and will hate one another. Then many false prophets will rise up and deceive many. And because lawlessness will abound, the love of many will grow cold. But he who endures to the end shall be saved. And this gospel of the kingdom will be preached in all the world as a witness to all the nations, and then the end will come.*

Some teachers sweep this passage away by declaring it only applied to the church prior to A.D. 70. Many passages of scripture had both an immediate application and a futurist application. Eschatology that claims to be victorious and then removes the cross so that victory is defined by not having to lay down your life should be suspect. Removing the cross always fails. We have transitioned from nation rising against nation, where we knew the location of the enemy, to kingdom against kingdom, where the enemy can be next door but bows and worships demons who are intent on killing anybody who is a Christian or a Jew. But in the midst of all this there is the promise of verse 14, *"And this gospel of the kingdom will be preached in all the world as a witness to all the nations, and then the end will come."* In the midst of all the persecution and all the war, it seems there is an anointing to live above it until a goal of witnessing the gospel in every nation is completed.

John 15:26-16:2 gives us further insight into kingdom against kingdom when it says, *"But when the Helper comes, whom I shall send to you from the Father, the Spirit of truth who proceeds from the Father, He will testify of Me. And you also will bear witness, because you have been with Me from the beginning. These things I have spoken to you, that you should not be made to stumble. They will put you out of the synagogues; yes, the time is coming that whoever kills you will think that he offers God service."* We are living in a time where, from mosque to mosque, people are being taught that whoever kills a Christian or a Jew is doing God service. While our Forefathers fought and died for a Christian nation and would not have tolerated radical Islam anywhere in the land, a perverse understanding of freedom of religion allows this cancer to grow in our midst. Christians in America need to wake up to the fact that persecution unto death is not that far away. It is being groomed in our very neighborhoods and is growing right under our noses. The church must rise up in a Kingly anointing and demand Throne-Room justice. If we fail to act, instead of gaining a harvest from Islam, we will become its victims. It is interesting to note that the church was begun in Priestly intercession for salvation, but to wind up the age, we must transition adding Kingly intercession for covenant justice!

Luke 23 records the Priestly intercession of Jesus as He was hanging on the cross. Verses 33-34 state, *"And when they had come to the place called Calvary, there they crucified Him, and the criminals, one on the right hand and the other on the left. Then Jesus said, 'Father, forgive them for they do not know what they do.' And they divided His garments and cast lots."* The prayer, *"Father, forgive them for they do not know what they do"* is the ultimate Priestly prayer. In Acts 7 where Paul is orchestrating the stoning of Stephen, we find this Priestly intercession is consistent with what Jesus modeled. Acts 7:59-60 states, *"And they stoned Stephen as he was calling on God and saying, 'Lord Jesus, receive my spirit.' Then he knelt down and cried out with a loud voice, 'Lord, do not charge them with this sin.' And when he had said this, he fell asleep."* Stephen fell asleep after he prayed, *"Lord, do not charge them with this sin."* That was ultimate Priestly intercession necessary for birthing the church age. Once Jesus ascended and took a seat as Judge of all the earth, another dimension of government was added! The end of the church age is very different from its beginning. The intercession of end-time martyrs reflects this transition.

Revelation chapter 5:6-8 states:

> *And I looked, and behold, in the midst of the throne and of the four living creatures, and in the midst of the elders, stood a Lamb as though it had been slain, having seven horns and seven eyes, which are the seven Spirits of God sent out into all the earth. Then He came and took the scroll out of the right hand of Him who sat on the throne. Now when He had taken the scroll, the four living creatures and the twenty-four elders fell down before the Lamb, each having a harp, and golden bowls full of incense which are the prayers of the saints.*

The question is, are the prayers of the saints in Revelation prayers for Priestly salvation or for Kingly justice? Verses 9-10 give us a clue, *"And they sang a new song, saying: 'You are worthy to take the scroll, And to open its seals; For You were slain, And have redeemed us to God by Your blood Out of every tribe and tongue and people and nation, And have made us kings and priests to our God; And we shall reign on the earth.'"* Verse 10 uses **bas-il-yooce** translated *"kings and priests"* in 10a but in 10b when it says, *"And we shall reign on the earth"* **bas-il-yoo-o** is used. **Bas-il-yooce** could be translated "kings" or "a kingdom of priests" as the noun, but **bas-il-yoo-o** as a verb cannot. There is a big difference if I am just one of a group of many who have a Kingly responsibility or an individual. In a group, I would yield to someone more qualified than I to shoulder the burden.

However, when we come to the verb it leaves us no wiggle room to escape. It says we shall do the action of a King and exercise Kingly authority. Every individual is responsible for action, meaning we must execute justice on the earth. It is obvious that the prayers of the saints are prayers for justice and there has been a transition. For those who might question this interpretation and think it arbitrary, we only have to go into chapter 6 and verses 9-10 to realize that the Priestly intercession of the saints has changed from the beginning of the church to a Kingly cry for justice. Verses 9-10 state, *"When He opened the fifth seal, I saw under the altar the souls of those who had been slain for the word of God and for the testimony which they held. And they cried with a loud voice, saying, 'How long, O Lord, holy and true, until You **judge** and **avenge** our blood on those who dwell on the earth?'"* In verse 10 the saints are not crying for salvation – they are crying for justice. Where are the heart cries for justice? The prayers of the saints are 99% Priestly, simply because the church has not been taught to enter the Kingly dimension. Religious freedoms our forefathers bought with blood are being stolen. The Kingly anointing will stop the thefts if we will but use it! The culture war is being lost by a church who refuses to unlock the armory through prayer!

In the process of presenting this truth a number of objections have come from those who remain exclusively in the Priestly mindset. One scripture often quoted as an objection is Luke 9:51-56:

> *Now it came to pass, when the time had come for Him to be received up, that He steadfastly set His face to go to Jerusalem, and sent messengers before His face. And as they went, they entered a village of the Samaritans, to prepare for Him. But they did not receive Him, because His face was set for the journey to Jerusalem. And when His disciples James and John saw this, they said, "Lord, do You want us to command fire to come down from heaven and consume them, just as*

Elijah did?" But He turned and rebuked them, and said, "You do not know what manner of spirit you are of. For the Son of Man did not come to destroy men's lives but to save them." And they went to another village.

The asterisks present in most Bibles indicate that neither the Nestle or the United Bible Society Greek texts include this verse. Many scholars believe this verse was added. The verse should read, *"But He rebuked them and they went to another village*." Now all we have to do is project what would have happened to the plan of salvation if James and John had called fire down on the Samaritans. How many people would have stood up to condemn Jesus with James and John ready to thunder fire from heaven upon them? Had they gotten their way, all of Israel would have heard about the Elijah-manifestation. The plan of salvation would have been thwarted. So it is obvious that *"knowing not what manner of spirit you are of"* even if it is included in the text, does **not** mean we cannot call for justice. What it means is we have to know the will of the Spirit in that moment. Verses 55-56 have been used as a club to impart guilt to anyone who dares to judge. When Jesus ascended, and was seated at the right Hand of God, He became the Judge of all the earth, making justice available. Every believer today is firmly persuaded that salvation is fully available when genuinely sought for anybody, anytime, day or night. Most Christians can lead someone to the Lord anytime they find a hearing ear. All of us accept and believe that salvation is fully available. We truly embrace the scripture as God's inerrant Word. Once we embrace the scripture as God's inerrant Word we are faced with a major transition from the beginning of the church age to the end of the church age.

This transition involves the emergence of a Kingly anointing for justice. We are told in Revelation chapter 11, verses 3-6:

"And I will give power to my two witnesses, and they will prophesy one thousand two hundred and sixty days, clothed in sackcloth." These are the two olive trees and the two lampstands standing before the God of the earth. And if anyone wants to harm them, fire proceeds from their mouth and devours their enemies. And if anyone wants to harm them, he must be killed in this manner. These have power to shut heaven, so that no rain falls in the days of their prophecy; and they have power over waters to turn them to blood, and to strike the earth with all plagues, as often as they desire.

These men walk in judgment on demand! The intensity of the situations they encounter determines the magnitude of judgment they dispense. Verse 6 clearly states, *"...as often as they desire."* If the two witnesses objected to this assignment and said, 'We want to save people. We cannot judge people,' what would Jesus say to them? He would likely say, 'It is not your choice! The assignment is, if the people are in opposition to MY will, and try to harm you, you must declare judgment on their heads!'

Intercession in the church changes from the beginning of the church age where it is mostly Priestly to the end of the church age where it is very, very Kingly. The real question for us right now is not whether we can grow into justice on demand, but can we even represent Jesus the Judge? Faith to act demands a biblical foundation. Our heart and our mind must agree that praying for judgment is God's revealed will. The church today has a dangerous deficit in God's Word! If we are confined in a Priestly mentality, we are incapable of representing Jesus the Judge. How much of the harvest will be lost because we refuse to qualify to participate with Jesus the Judge? Knowing Jesus as Savior allows us to represent Jesus the Savior. Knowing Jesus as Giver of the Holy Spirit allows us to minister the Spirit. Knowing Jesus the Healer releases us to pray for healing. Knowing Jesus the Prophet releases faith to prophesy. Knowing Jesus the Judge releases faith to pray judgment. Peter did it. Paul did it. Mordecai Ham did it. We can as well! Declare war on the faith deficit. Know and walk with Jesus the Judge.

Will you move with dominion
And Spirit-led power?
Are you readied and listening
For the right day and hour?

Jayne Houghton

Chapter 7

Justice to Victory

Jesus took justice to victory as a major assignment guaranteeing our access to the King's anointing. Matthew 12:14-21 states:

> *Then the Pharisees went out and took counsel against Him, how they might destroy Him. But when Jesus knew it, He withdrew from there; and great multitudes followed Him, and He healed them all. And He warned them not to make Him known, that it might be fulfilled which was spoken by Isaiah the prophet, saying: "Behold, My Servant whom I have chosen, My Beloved in whom My soul is well pleased; I will put My Spirit upon Him, And He will declare justice to the Gentiles. He will not quarrel nor cry out, Nor will anyone hear His voice in the streets. A bruised reed He will not break, And smoking flax He will not quench, Till He sends forth justice to victory. And in His name Gentiles will trust."*

It is obvious from this passage that one of the major assignments Jesus accomplished was taking justice to victory. What value is that to us? Jesus took our sin – I know the value of that. He took our sickness – I know the value of that. He took our pain – I know the value of that. He took our grief – I know the value of that. He took our sorrow – I know the value of that. He took our rebellion – I know the value of that. He took our injustice – What is the value of that? Verse 18 makes it clear there is an assignment of the Holy Spirit to manifest justice, when

He says, *"...I will put My Spirit upon Him, And He will declare justice to the Gentiles."* We have been content to relegate justice to a Priestly application.

A major assignment of the Holy Spirit is bringing justice. We have not been taught applications of the Spirit outside of the Priestly cry for salvation. Today's church has yet to embrace the promises of the Holy Spirit in the light of manifesting the Kingly anointing in bringing forth God's justice. In John 16:7-11 it states,

> *Nevertheless I tell you the truth. It is to your advantage that I go away; for if I do not go away, the Helper will not come to you; but if I depart, I will send Him to you. And when He has come, He will convict the world of sin, and of righteousness, and of judgment: of sin, because they do not believe in Me; of righteousness, because I go to My Father and you see Me no more; of judgment, because the ruler of this world is judged.*

The Holy Spirit has a job to *"...convict the world of sin, of righteousness and of judgment."* It is interesting that righteousness and judgment are the governmental issues for the kingdom of David and go directly to the foundation of God's Throne. It should not be a surprise nor should we gloss over the fact that Jesus made it apparent that some of this would be hidden until He finished the plan of salvation. Verses 12-13 allude to the fact that once the mission is accomplished the latter part would unfold, *"I still have many things to say to you, but you cannot bear them now. However, when He, the Spirit of truth, has come, He will guide you into all truth; for He will not speak on His own authority, but whatever He hears He will speak; and He will tell you things to come."* Jesus made it clear that justice is a manifestation of the Spirit and those who walk in the Spirit will demonstrate that justice more and more until on-demand is a reality. According to Revelation it will become more and more pronounced as we move into the end-times. (If you are a preterist and believe Revelation was completed in A.D. 70, why are you not walking in this now?)

Jesus did not have Matthew to quote from. He was speaking out of Isaiah chapter 42 and perhaps if we go to the original source in Isaiah, it will shed some light on the justice to victory issue. Isaiah 42:1-3 states, *"Behold! My Servant whom I uphold, My Elect One in whom My soul delights! I have put My Spirit upon Him; He will bring forth justice to the Gentiles. He will not cry out, nor raise His voice, Nor cause His voice to be heard in the street. A bruised reed He will not break, And smoking flax He will not quench; He will bring forth justice for truth."* The justice to victory in Matthew is actually justice for truth in Isaiah 42:3. The Hebrew word for justice in verse 3 is **mish-pawt**. A **mish-pawt** was the prophetic proclamation of a **shaw-fat** who was a judge. Samuel was a judge whose prophetic proclamations did not fall to the ground because God brought every one of them to pass. Samuel's life-style choices of righteousness brought justice to Israel for 40 years. Eli's standard of unrighteousness denied justice to Israel for 40 years.

Every Priest has to proclaim justice based on the righteous standards of God's Word. What verse 3 promises is that Jesus bought and paid for access to divine justice based on the moral standard of God's Word or His truth **eh-meth.** **Eh-meth** means firmness, faithfulness or truth. Truth is the body of ethical and religious knowledge as revealed in scripture. When judges and politicians vote or rally to protect homosexual marriage or abortion, every believer who has a righteous foundation should access God's justice. Just as God cut off Herod, He can cut off judges, senators, representatives and even preachers. What we have done as a church is consistently prayed **for** the salvation of that judge or leader. But when such prayers are not Spirit-led, it enables them to continue in their sinful ways and moves our land toward destruction. There comes a time when the church has to say, enough! God have mercy on the nation, and cut off the politician or judge. Let the judge be JUDGED by the JUDGE OF ALL THE EARTH.

Jesus made justice accessible based on the atonement. Verses 4-6 of Isaiah 42 declare God's purpose in this process:

> *He will not fail nor be discouraged, Till He has established justice in the earth; And the coastlands shall wait for His law. Thus says God the LORD, Who created the heavens and stretched them out, Who spread forth the earth and that which comes from it. Who gives breath to the people on it, And spirit to those who walk on it: I, the LORD, have called You in righteousness, And will hold Your hand; I will keep You and give You as a covenant to the people, As a light to the Gentiles...*

Jesus has been given to us as a covenant, a covenant guaranteeing both Priestly salvation and Kingly justice.

Perhaps we need to see the attitude of God when justice does not prevail in the land. Isaiah 59 gives us this insight in verses 11b-15:

> *...We look for justice, but there is none; For salvation, but it is far from us. For our transgressions are multiplied before You, And our sins testify against us; For our transgressions are with us, And as for our iniquities, we know them: In transgressing and lying against the LORD, And departing from our God, Speaking oppression and revolt, Conceiving and uttering from the heart words of falsehood. Justice is turned back, And righteousness stands afar off; For truth is fallen in the street, And equity cannot enter. So truth fails, And he who departs from evil makes himself a prey. Then the LORD saw it, and it displeased Him That there was no justice.*

When verse 15 says the LORD saw there was no justice and it displeased Him, that is a very mild rendering of the Hebrew. When there is no justice, it is evil in God's eyes. **There comes a point where continually praying salvation for wayward and wicked judges is evil in the sight of the Lord because all we are doing is enabling them.**

David never prayed for the traitorous Ahithophel's salvation. He prayed for his judgment and got it! Why enable demonized judges to continue perverting the land? Unsanctified mercy because of a Priestly mindset aids evil. Demons love it because it gives them freedom to destroy! In Isaiah 59 when a religious culture perverts justice Jesus might say to everyone praying salvation on these judges, "You don't know what spirit you are of. Your discernment is zero. You are dumber than dust. You are enabling people to destroy the land when you should be following the Spirit and praying justice on them and for their utter, total and complete removal." We know Jesus meant what He said in Isaiah 59 because verses 17-19 state:

> *For He put on righteousness as a breastplate, And a helmet of salvation on His head; He put on the garments of vengeance for clothing, And was clad with zeal as a cloak. According to their deeds, accordingly He will repay, Fury to His adversaries, Recompense to His enemies; The coastlands He will fully repay. So shall they fear The name of the LORD from the west, And His glory from the rising of the sun; When the enemy comes in like a flood, The Spirit of the LORD will lift up a standard against him.*

Where is the standard? Where is the fear of the Lord? The fear of the Lord comes *after* Ananias and Sapphira events! The fear of the Lord comes when the church moves God to remove a 'Herod'! The fear of the Lord comes when we declare the judgment of blindness on an

'Elymas' and God performs it!

The primary exegetical principle has always been, first and foremost, "Context determines meaning." The context of *"When the enemy comes in like a flood, The Spirit of the LORD will lift up a standard against him"* is not Priestly salvation. It is the restoration of biblical justice! We have interpreted that in the light of the Jesus we know from the gospels. We must allow it to stand in its context in Isaiah 59 and declare what it really means! When the Lord sees there is no justice for the unborn – fifty million murdered aborted children – it is evil in His sight. How dare we continue enabling those judges, when we should be declaring, prophesying and decreeing divine justice. Let the Hand of the Lord remove them. The average citizen can demand justice any day of the week and eventually get results. A pastor in the Seattle area told me an account of their family physician when she was a child

. Just after *Roe v. Wade* made abortion legal, this family physician became one of the first doctors in the nation to advertise abortion available in his office. My pastor friend's Catholic mother was outraged and changed physicians. She visited clinics to encourage women to keep their babies. She prayed for justice. The doctor fell from a horse and hit his head on a rock and died. My friend's Catholic mother sat her children down and said to them, "You don't mess around with God's stuff, the doctor got his justice!" Will the church ever take off their Priestly blinders and meet the Jesus who is the Judge of all the earth and represent Him for Who He IS in the last days? I trust we will! Thirty years ago a Catholic mother had more success moving God's Hand than most of us who stand in pulpits today. No Christian can make peace with evil and bring the justice of God. Jesus took justice to victory! Let's enforce it!

Unsanctified mercy
Enabling what's evil
Produces a cowardice
In kind like a weasel!

While justice and courage
to make war and prevail
Cause victory to rise
And will evil derail!

Jayne Houghton

Chapter 8

Jesus and Lawlessness

We are so familiar with Jesus as Savior that we often fail to realize that He pronounced judgment on lawlessness and was very specific about its application. In Matthew 7 He warned about being overcome by a spirit of mammon (for a complete exposé see *Purifying the Altar*). Verses 15-16 state, *"Beware of false prophets, who come to you in sheep's clothing, but inwardly they are ravenous wolves. You will know them by their fruits. Do men gather grapes from thornbushes or figs from thistles?"* Jesus made it clear that we do not judge people necessarily by what they preach, although preaching has to line up with scripture, but by the fruit they leave behind. In verses 21-23 Jesus laid down a judgment, *"Not everyone who says to Me, 'Lord, Lord,' shall enter the kingdom of heaven, but he who does the will of My Father in heaven. Many will say to Me in that day, 'Lord, Lord, have we not prophesied in Your name, cast out demons in Your name, and done many wonders in Your name?' And then I will declare to them, 'I never knew you; depart from Me, you who practice lawlessness!'"* Imagine the level of deception necessary to capture a minister who moves in the gifts of the Spirit. How can we prophesy, cast out demons, and do wonders while worshipping demons? The only spirit strong enough to execute such captivity is the same spirit of mammon that angered Jesus. When Jesus challenged mammon by cleaning house in the temple in Mark 11, the rulers responded with crucifixion.

In Matthew 13:41 Jesus specifically states He will send angels to remove those who practice lawlessness. In Matthew 24:12 Jesus warned, *"And because lawlessness will abound, the love of many will grow cold."* Jesus would probably say to most churches today exactly what He said in Matthew 23. You've done a great job in preaching tithe and offering but you have neglected *"...the weightier matters of the law."* Verse 23 states, *"Woe to you, scribes and Pharisees, hypocrites! For you pay tithe of mint and anise and cumin, and have neglected the weightier matters of the law: justice and mercy and faith. These you ought to have done, without leaving the others undone."*

Jesus said the first order of business for a believer after embracing righteousness was to carry and be an agent of God's justice. As agents of God's justice, we also have to minister mercy. This agrees with what Revelation 1:5-6 states about Jesus making us first Kings and second Priests, first justice and then mercy. It takes faith to walk in both. God sent a faith movement. Many in that movement squandered revelation by using it for personal gain rather than bringing God's justice and learning to extend His mercy. The seed was hijacked. When our primary application of revelation is for personal gain, we forfeit a generational transfer for a trip to the Promised Land and continue to wander around in Egypt. Using faith for our own advancement rather than using faith for God's purpose is detrimental.

Amos 5 describes a religious environment where God does not even want to hear our worship because we are not doing justice. Amos 5:21-24 states, *"I hate, I despise your feast days, And I do not savor your sacred assemblies. Though you offer Me burnt offerings and your grain offerings, I will not accept them, Nor will I regard your fattened peace offerings. Take away from Me the noise of your songs, For I will not hear the melody of your stringed instruments. But let justice run down like water, And righteousness like a mighty stream."* Is it possible to become so side-tracked by personal gain and by building one's own ministry, that the Lord looks at the church service and says, "I hate it. I'm not coming. It is an abomination. If you want My Presence, make a decision that you will become an agent of justice."

Perhaps *The Message* Bible says it best in verses 21 -24 when it states:

> *I can't stand your religious meetings. I'm fed up with your conferences and conventions. I want nothing to do with your religion projects, your pretentious slogans and goals. I'm sick of your fund-raising schemes, your public relations and image making. I've had all I can take of your noisy ego-music. When was the last time you sang to Me? Do you know what I want? I want justice – oceans of it. I want fairness – rivers of it. That's what I want. That's all I want.*

The major theme of scripture is salvation, but salvation demands justice. God is the Author of both. The foundations of His Throne are justice and righteousness. Psalm 89 makes very clear Who we are dealing with in verses 13-14, *"You have a mighty arm; Strong is Your hand, and high is Your right hand. Righteousness and justice are the foundation of Your throne; Mercy and truth go before Your face."* Over and over again in scripture we are told about righteousness and justice. Psalm 97:1-3 states, *"The LORD reigns; Let the earth rejoice; Let the multitude of isles be glad! Clouds and darkness surround Him; Righteousness and justice are the foundation of His throne. A fire goes before Him, And burns up His enemies round about."* God is the God of justice and justice proceeds from Who He IS. The church is commissioned as an agent of justice and salvation. We administer Priestly salvation but we balk at ministering Kingly justice. Justice to a Priest manifests in salvation. Justice to a King manifests in judgment.

Go with pure and humble heart
and with My unction too.
Go and pray at My command,
and I will go with you!

Jayne Houghton

Chapter 9

Justice in the Atonement

As we trace the atoning work of the priests, Exodus 29:36-37 says, *"...and you shall offer a bull every day as a sin offering for atonement. You shall cleanse the altar when you make atonement for it, and you shall anoint it to sanctify it. Seven days you shall make atonement for the altar and sanctify it. And the altar shall be most holy. Whatever touches the altar must be holy."* In chapter 30, verse 10, we find, *"And Aaron shall make atonement upon its horns once a year with the blood of the sin offering of atonement; once a year he shall make atonement upon it throughout your generations. It is most holy to the LORD."* The issue of atonement is the issue of offering a blood sacrifice in place of a person for their sin and iniquity and so it is covered for a year under the dispensation of the Old Covenant. God taught the people there is no atonement without the shedding of blood and the atonement means being made at one with God through the blood sacrifice in place of our sin.

God progressively prepared Israel to receive their Messiah through what would be the ultimate atoning sacrifice so that what He bought would be purchased by one sacrifice forever and every generation would have access who would acknowledge Jesus as Lord. Isaiah 53 is the principle atonement chapter outlining everything Jesus bought and paid for when He died for us. Isaiah 53:1-4 states

Who has believed our report? And to whom has the arm of the LORD been revealed? For He shall grow up before Him as a tender plant, And as a root out of dry ground. He has no form or comeliness; And when we see Him, There is no beauty that we should desire Him. He is despised and rejected by men, A Man of sorrows and acquainted with grief. And we hid, as it were, our faces from Him; He was despised, and we did not esteem Him. Surely He has borne our griefs And carried our sorrows; Yet we esteemed Him stricken, Smitten by God, and afflicted."

In verse 4 the issues of atonement are outlined. The Hebrew word translated *"griefs"* is **khol-ee** and it is used twenty-four times in the Old Testament. It is translated as sickness twelve times and disease seven times. It should be obvious that the first issue of the atonement which Jesus took upon Himself was sickness. Most of us believe that Jesus took sickness upon Himself in order to guarantee healing for His church. The early church made healing a central part of their belief and practice. It is obvious that it continued through the centuries because at one point in the Roman Empire the argument against persecuting the Christians was that they were the ones who healed the sick.

How can we selectively accept one part of what Jesus bought and paid for and fully dismiss another? It is time for the church to dramatically commit and believe God for every element of the atonement in manifestation, since it has already been bought and paid for! The Hebrew word translated *"sorrow"* is **mak-obe**. It only has sixteen occurrences in the Old Testament and it can apply to physical or mental sorrow, grief or pain. Jesus not only took sickness upon Himself but He took grief, pain, and agony. Isaiah 53:5 goes on to say, *"But He was wounded for our transgressions, He was bruised for our iniquities; The chastisement for our peace was upon Him, And by His stripes we are healed."* It is really hard to argue with verse 5 seeing that it fully describes the exchange God intended for everyone who confesses Jesus as Lord. Isaiah 53:6 says, *"All we like sheep have gone astray; We have turned every one, to his own way; And the LORD has laid on Him the iniquity of us all."* Not a single Christian who understands anything about foundational biblical truths has any argument with Isaiah 53:6. We can all say we have been like sheep and gone astray and done our own thing, but the LORD laid our sin on Jesus and redeemed us. This is cornerstone, foundational gospel 101. There is no contest. We have no argument with Isaiah 53:7, *"He was oppressed and He was afflicted, Yet He opened not His mouth; He was led as a lamb to the slaughter, And as a sheep before its shearers is silent, So He opened not his mouth."* Jesus taught and practiced "turn the other check Christianity" while He was birthing salvation, but in Revelation no cheek is turned because He is judging and making war!

Much of the book of Revelation is about the ascended Christ and what He does from heaven sovereignly through the church who is His witness. The book of Revelation marks a dramatic transition in the ministry of Jesus. This same transition appears in Isaiah 53:8 which says, *"He was taken from prison and from* [**mish-pawt**] *judgment, And who will declare His generation? For He was cut off from the land of the living; For the transgressions of My people He was stricken."* Verse 8 makes it crystal clear there are two more elements here bought and paid for in the atonement of Jesus, but these two the church has neglected. Jesus took all injustice upon Himself, guaranteeing our access to Throne-Room justice and because He was cut off from the land of the living, He guarantees our covenant access to justice, cutting off the enemy from the land of the living when the enemy is hindering our assigned harvest. Covenant justice is in the atonement. Mordecai Ham understood this and practiced it a hundred years ago. Let the recovery begin.

"Turn-the-other-cheek" Christianity can be a powerful weapon in winning the lost and changing society, but it can at the wrong time forfeit a victory Jesus wants to gain. Matthew 5 dominates the thinking of the church today but biblical balance demands we develop the anointing for justice. "Turn-the-other-cheek" Christianity has been made to cover much more ground and territory than it really should if we set it in the context of Jesus preparing His disciples for the Kingdom. Verses 1-2 indicate preparation, *"And seeing the multitudes, He went up on a mountain, and when He was seated* ***His disciples*** *came to Him. Then He opened His mouth and taught them, saying:"* The Sermon on the Mount is discipleship training for winning covenant people because when Jesus sends them out in Matthew chapter 10:5b-6 He tells them two places not to go and then one place to go. He tells them, *"Do not go into the way of the Gentiles, and do not enter a city of the Samaritans. But go rather to the lost sheep of the house of Israel."* Matthew chapter 5 begins with the Beatitudes and then transitions to the Similitudes. Verse 13 is the first Similitude and it is very important in setting the context for what has become "turn-the-other-cheek" Christianity. Verse 13 is a key. It says, *"You are the salt of the earth; but if the salt loses its flavor, how shall it be seasoned? It is then* ***good*** *for nothing but to be thrown out and trampled under foot by men."* Jesus said *"You are salt..."* Salt was a preservative but it was also a sign of the covenant. The priests were commanded to salt every sacrifice because salt was a form of the covenant and it brought the worshipper into covenant fulfillment with everything that God offered. Leviticus 2:13 tells us, *"And every offering of your grain offering you shall season with salt; you shall not allow the salt of the covenant of your God to be lacking from your grain offering. With all your offerings you shall offer salt."* Because every offering had to be offered with salt, every believing individual then became God's form of salt in their country, kindred, and culture. The very three things that Abram was called to leave – country, kindred, and culture – had an enthroned purpose. The goal was to establish a new country, a new kindred, and a new biblical culture. The yardstick for measuring God's salt, in those three arenas, is our ability to access the anointing to preserve or recover country, kindred, and culture.

The key to understanding this verse is in the phrase, "It is then **good** for nothing..." and has already been explained by looking at **is-khoo-o**. The *Greek English Dictionary of the New Testament* defines **is-khoo-o** as, "be able, can, every source win over, defeat, be strong, grow strong" and emphasizes the issue of overcoming in a contest. The example of Elijah is given because of how he preserved the nation. Elijah did not turn the other cheek to governmental evil. Elijah had enough salt to pray an agrarian economy into bankruptcy by withholding rain for three and one-half years in order to cleanse the land. The prophets of Baal were destroyed. Judgment saved the nation. He prayed again in verse 18 and released the economy. This scripture says *"...and the earth produced its fruit."* Jesus said that we should have enough salt to be able to pray and move God's Hand to dry up resources that support evil. Jesus demonstrated that salt by cleaning house in the temple. Your prayers can also clean house! If the news media companies only 'selectively' report facts and twist truth to the detriment of the Kingdom, then we have a responsibility to pray them into bankruptcy. If the Spirit leads us to pray this and we do not, then we are really a saltless people. Jesus taught "turn-the-other-cheek" Christianity in the context of being a people of salt. The Bible defines a person of salt as one who has the ability to covenantally bankrupt that which supports evil. Having salt is bringing judgment on organizations that if left **unchecked would destroy the society.**

Jesus taught a message of the Kingdom in Matthew 11:11-12, *"Assuredly, I say to you, among those born of women there has not risen one greater than John the Baptist; but he who is least in the kingdom of heaven is greater than he. And from the days of John the Baptist until now the kingdom of heaven suffers violence, and the violent take it by force."* According to Jesus any New Testament believer should be able to do what an Old Testament prophet did, since John the Baptist was the greatest of the prophets, which included Elijah and Elisha. The least in the New Testament Kingdom is greater than John the Baptist. James believed Jesus and used Elijah as an example of what prayer should accomplish in the life of a New Testament believer. Those of us who stand in the pulpit and minister mush and milk toast when losing a nation will give an account. If we never teach the difference between the holy and the profane, nor teach the covenant platform that enables a person to have biblical covenantal salt and to make a difference in their culture, their country and their kindred, woe is us! We will give an account in eternity for not empowering the church to gain the promised harvest. There should be enough salt in the church to bring the evil media corporations to bankruptcy. Every major media company who leavens the culture of the land into destruction should face the salt of God's church. They should see the fruit of a salty church bringing God's Hand to bear on their business until at the end of three and a half years they have no dollars and have gained an ear to hear.

What Bible School equips the church to walk with Jesus the Judge? Where can we go to learn how to be a salty covenantal people? One day we are going to give an account for how we used the salt we have. "Turn-the-other-cheek" Christianity applies the principle of nonviolent social resistance. Jesus would seriously rebuke a believer for even thinking of shooting an abortion doctor. **Our weapon of war is prayer!** Being salt means moving God's Hand against the enemy! Anything less steals the thunder of the church. It is an assault against the very identity of who we are in Christ. Jesus taught this under the umbrella of having salt, and having salt means having it like Elijah did. Today's believers have been taught to make "turn-the-other-cheek" the standard in every situation. Representing only the Priestly Jesus makes us effectively powerless against evil. And Mighty King and Savior Jesus was not, in any way, powerless against evil!

Every Christian must be willing to follow the Holy Spirit into the Priestly or into the Kingly mode as led. Many a circumstance and situation will demand going Priestly or "turn-the-other-cheek" in order to win that individual, but never at the expense of losing a country, kindred, or culture. In the last hundred years we have seen this passage dominate the church to the point it is so far out of balance that we are in dire danger of losing our country, kindred, and culture, because no one will execute Kingly justice. We are too busy "turning the other cheek." Segments of the church openly tolerate evil. Is it any wonder that Paul said we need to *"...study to show ourselves approved to God, workmen that need not to be ashamed, rightly dividing the word of truth"* (2 Timothy 2:15). A hundred years of preachers are liable to be *"ashamed"* for elevating this passage out of its context and taking a sword away from the church. It is time to reverse course, return these principles to balance in the Holy Spirit, and prepare ourselves and a generation for the days ahead.

A consistent theme of scripture is justice, and when God does not see it He is displeased! Jesus did not "turn-the-other-cheek" to evil. "Turn-the-other-cheek" Christianity has become an excuse for passivity in the face of evil. When ministers choose not to confront sin, justifying by phrases like, "I'm a bridge-builder" or "I'm a uniter not a divider," they stand in danger of being more seeker-sensitive than they are Holy Spirit-sensitive. The greatest threat to any nation is not terrorism, communism, or Islam, but pastors in pulpits viewing cultural decline with passivity. Most New Testament Christians do not attend a church that fully teaches covenant truth. Because they do not know their covenant, they are locked in Priestly garments and are losing everything that previous generations bought and paid for in religious freedom. Jesus said we would know individuals by their fruit. The methods of the early church were confrontation unto death. And their fruit was lives saved and Kingdom purposes preserved. The methods of today's church are mostly passivity in the face of evil, ignorance of scripture and so much unsanctified mercy that many Christians are nicer than God Himself. And what is the fruit? It is the undermining of Kingdom purposes by evil, leading to a once-Godly land filling a cup of iniquity at an unprecedented rate.

God has never been opposed to judging and destroying to save the land. The Bible is full of such divine interventions in answer to prayer. But the religious church keeps evil-doers in place and enables them to continue unchecked by praying Priestly prayers instead of Judicial ones. This is something David would never have done. Paul would have thought such behavior lunacy and had he prayed Priestly instead of Kingly, Peter's life might have been lost before his time without judicial prayers to remove Herod. Let us break free from tradition and begin representing the Kingly Christ as the New Testament church did!

They called forth My justice,
Those prophets of old.
Are you counted among
The wise and the bold?

Jayne Houghton

Chapter 10

Cutting off the Enemy

The only place in the New Testament where a minister is translated highlights the defining of Isaiah 53:8. It is the passage where Philip is translated so that he can minister to the Ethiopian eunuch. Acts 8:30-33 states:

> *So Phillip ran to him, and heard him reading the prophet Isaiah, and said, "Do you understand what you are reading?" And he said, "How can I, unless someone guides me?" And he asked Philip to come up and sit with him. The place in the Scripture which he read was this: "He was led as a sheep to the slaughter; And like a lamb silent before its shearer, So He opened not His mouth. In His humiliation His justice was taken away. And who will declare His generation? For His life is taken from the earth."*

Jesus not only took our sin upon Himself, He took all injustice on Himself and was "cut off" guaranteeing our access to Kingly justice and the ability and anointing to move the Hand of God to "cut off" the enemy when injustice hinders a harvest.

There are five Theocratic Covenants culminating in the New Covenant and every single one of them carries the promise to "cut off" our enemies. If we are so valuable to God that Jesus was willing to die to save us, **then are we not valuable enough that He will kill to deliver**

and preserve us? Each of us must look in the mirror of scripture and ask ourselves these questions. Am I valuable enough to God for His Son to die to save me? Am I valuable enough to God that He will kill to preserve me so that I can finish my race? Even if your race ends in martyrdom, it should end on God's terms not the enemy's. Jesus was martyred but the enemy tried to take His life on two occasions prior to when He laid it down. By exercising covenantal authority, Jesus finished His race. Will God "cut off" our enemies when we stand on the covenant? The answer is "Yes," and our prayer life has to change! The obvious question is how do we invoke covenant to "cut off" the enemy?

If there is any hesitation in our hearts, then it is obvious that a distinct lack of biblical foundation exists in understanding covenant. Everything that God has done with man He has done by establishing covenant so we can know what to expect and what He will do. In Genesis 15:7-8 we view an exchange between God and Abram from which comes the heart-cry of all mankind and the answer to that heart-cry immediately follows. Verses 7-8 state, *"Then He said to him, 'I am the LORD, who brought you out of Ur of the Chaldeans, to give you this land to inherit it.' And he said, 'Lord GOD, how shall I know that I will inherit it?'"* God promised land but Abram said words are not enough, I want more. I want to ***know*** that I am going to inherit it. I want something stronger than just Your promise. And God's answer was a blood covenant. There are five Theocratic Covenants in scripture that pertain to the rule of God where He has promised to judge our enemies. All five of these covenants have threads that run through them that are just as good today as they were when Abraham was walking the earth. The hesitancy to access Throne-Room justice that Jesus bought and paid for can possibly be attributed to a simple lack of foundation in covenant. If that is the case then it is time to erase that deficit in understanding by following these judicial threads through each of the Theocratic

Covenants.

The first Theocratic (pertaining to the rule of God) Covenant is offered to Abraham. In Genesis 12:1-3 we are told:

> *Now the LORD had said to Abram: "Get out of your country, From your kindred And from your father's house, To a land that I will show you. I will make you a great nation; I will bless you And make your name great; And you shall be a blessing. I will bless those who bless you, And I will curse him who curses you; And in you all the families of the earth shall be blessed."*

The Abrahamic Covenant has a judicial component, *"...and I will curse him who curses you..."* The question is, did God mean if necessary He would destroy our enemies if we stand on covenant? In Genesis 20 Sarah is in Abimelech's tent and God visits Abimelech and says to him in verse 7, *"Now therefore, restore the man's wife; for he is a prophet, and he will pray for you and you shall live. But if you do not restore her, know that you shall surely die, you and all who are yours."* **If we are so valuable that Jesus was willing to die to save us, will He not kill to preserve us?** Is God willing to cut off your enemy? He certainly was for Abraham because it was part of the covenant. Galatians 3:29 states, if we are Christ's, we are heirs! If we participate in the Abrahamic Covenant, according to Galatians, then know assuredly that we have a right to ask God to cut off the enemy! "Turn-the-other-cheek" is a powerful weapon in offering life to pre-Christians but as we approach the end of the age, opposition by evil forces grows dramatically, demanding a balanced biblical approach to preparation. One key to this balance is Acts 15 and the Lord's promise to rebuild the Tabernacle of David which translates into the heart of David being reproduced in a generation of believers. The core concepts expressed and released before the Ark in intercessory Psalms demanded covenant death and destruction on the enemy so the promised-land could be possessed. There are many enemies to the harvest, and some of them must be cut off to possess the promise. A second key to the Kingdom which perfectly reflects David's heart-cry is the justice-on-demand promised to the witnesses in Revelation. This seems to signify a transition from emphasizing salvation to justice in manifestation forced by the steadfast refusal to repent! As the gospel is preached in every nation, accountability arises demanding justice. Many leaders act as if there is no God and no standard of divine justice. The Holy Spirit has the assignment of convincing people of judgment, but unless the church manifests it there are no examples to bring conviction. By abandoning covenant we forfeit the foundation upon which we stand to demand judgment. By learning the covenant, the church gains a platform from which justice can be executed! The church has been too busy "turning-the-other cheek" to ask for covenant victory. May the church grow into the power of the covenant necessary to confront the depth of evil we are facing!

Galatians 3:26-29 says, *"For you are all sons of God through faith in Christ Jesus. For as many of you as were baptized into Christ have put on Christ. There is neither Jew nor Greek, there is neither slave nor free, there is neither male nor female; for you are all one in Christ Jesus. And if you are Christ's, then you are Abraham's seed, and heirs according to the promise."* The best dictionary for the Bible is the Bible. If we simply allow scripture to define itself we cannot go wrong. We may even grow into something. According to Galatians, the Abrahamic covenant belongs to us in Christ. We have access to a covenant that guarantees God Himself will move in our behalf and cut off the enemy. Jesus Christ is the same yesterday, today and forever!

In Exodus 19 God offered a second Theocratic Covenant to the entire nation of Israel to make them all priests. This became the Mosaic Covenant. In chapter 20 when they found out what it was really going to cost because God came to them and thundered out the Ten Commandments, great fear came on them and they said in effect, "Moses, we'll pay you. You go meet with God and find out what He says and come tell us." The clergy laity system was born. Nevertheless, the second Theocratic Covenant established God's moral standard. The question is, when God gave the Ten Commandments does the Mosaic Covenant give us access to God's justice to the point that He will cut off our enemies? Exodus 23:20-23 says:

> *Behold, I send an Angel before you to keep you in the way and to bring you into the place which I have prepared. Beware of Him and obey His voice; do not provoke Him, for He will not pardon your transgressions; for My name is in Him. But if you indeed obey His voice and do all that I speak, then I will be an enemy to your enemies and an adversary to your adversaries. For My Angel will go before you and bring you in to the Amorites and the Hittities and the Perizzites and the Canaanites and the Hivites and the Jebusites; and* ***I will cut them off****.*

The Mosaic Covenant provided for the execution and removal of enemies just like God promised Abram.

In Deuteronomy 30 God made a covenant with Israel promising them land. The covenant for the land was a guarantee and further manifestation of what God had spoken to Abraham. It appears in Deuteronomy 30:11-20. Verses 15-16 state, *"See, I have set before you today life and good, death and evil, in that I command you today to love the LORD your God, to walk in His ways, and to keep His commandments, His statutes, and His judgments, that you may live and multiply; and the LORD your God will bless you in the land which you go to possess."*

What magnitude of blessing could they expect when facing an enemy to possess their land? In Joshua 10 we get a glimpse. God rains down hailstones on their enemy and so more are killed by the hail than by Israel. Verse 11 states, *"And it happened, as they fled before Israel and were on the descent of Beth Horon, that the LORD cast down large hailstones from heaven on them as far as Azekah, and they died. There were more who died from the hailstones than those whom the children of Israel killed with the sword."*

This is where Joshua, encouraged by God, says, let the sun and the moon stand still for about a day until we utterly destroy the enemy. You can almost feel Joshua saying, "There is no way, God, You are going to kill more than we are." And God stopped the rotation of the planets so that covenant vengeance could be taken on the enemy. Is God committed to preserving Israel's land? The covenant still works. It is obvious that the covenant promising Israel land allows people to pray, and God will remove those who are attempting to steal their God-given inheritance. We would hope that America's national leaders would get to know the Theocratic Covenants and stop the stupidity of trying to offer land for peace. Jesus never negotiated with demons! Why should we? It does not work! Pushing Israel to give up land against the covenant is like spitting in God's face. Miriam tried it but was not very successful! Numbers 12:13,14 says, *"So Moses cried out to the Lord, saying, 'Please heal her, O God, I pray!' Then the Lord said to Moses, 'If her father had but spit in her face, would she not be shamed seven days? Let her be shut out of the camp seven days, and afterward she may be received again.'"*

The fourth of the Theocratic Covenants is the "Sure Mercies of David" offered in 2 Samuel chapter 7. In verse 9 God said, *"And I have been with you wherever you have gone, and have cut off all your enemies from before you, and have made you a great name, like the name of the great men who are on the earth."* We know by David's own example in Psalm 143 that his covenant included the cutting off of his enemies and that God did it. On his way out of Jerusalem when Absalom had taken power, David prayed covenant mercy for the land. In verses 11-12 he said, *"Revive me, O LORD, for Your name's sake! For Your righteousness' sake bring my soul out of trouble. In Your mercy* ***cut off*** *my enemies. And destroy all those who afflict my soul; For I am Your servant."* That is a Godly biblical judicial prayer uttered covenantally out of the mouth of David and God and honoring covenant brought it to pass, not with one spear, not with two spears, but three spears in the heart of Absalom – one for every One of the Trinity. God is a Covenant Maker and a Covenant Keeper to a thousand generations. The same God who died to save us is willing to kill to preserve us! We must allow the Spirit to lead in this application, but this covenant promise is suffering from lack of use!

In the New Testament we see the manifestations. In Acts chapter 12 when Herod stretches out his hand and kills James and jails Peter the church begins to pray. An angel is sent and Peter is released. Then in verses 21-23 we have biblical justice. 'The weight of how you touch My people is the weight of how I will touch you!' The Greek word **ax-ee-os** describes this principle in the New Testament. This word describes God's principle of justice from the Old Covenant to the New and it governs the dispensing of all justice in the book of Revelation. Acts 12:21-23 states, *"So on a set day Herod, arrayed in royal apparel, sat on his throne and gave an oration to them. And the people kept shouting, 'The voice of a god and not of a man!' Then immediately an angel of the Lord struck him, because he did not give glory to God. And he was eaten by worms and died."* Biblical justice with the ability to cut off the enemy is a thread that runs through every major Theocratic Covenant. Why have we abandoned justice and why are we extending unsanctified mercy to Supreme Court justices, senators, representatives and even presidents who are filling our land with iniquity when we should be asking God to cut them off. Where are today's Davids? Where is the restoration of the tabernacle of David which guarantees this heart in action? This first Psalm that David prayed before the Ark when he brought it into Jerusalem in 1 Chronicles 16 contains a very familiar scripture to most of us but it has been so watered down by tradition that it has taken on an entirely different meaning. Verses 7 and 14-22 state:

> *And on that day David first delivered this psalm into the hand of Asaph and his brethren, to thank the LORD... He is the LORD our God; His judgments are in all the earth. Remember His covenant always, The word which He commanded, for a thousand generations, The covenant which He made with Abraham, And His oath to Isaac, And confirmed it to Jacob for a statute, To Israel for an everlasting covenant, Saying, "To you I will give the land of Canaan As the allotment of your inheritance." When you were but few in number, Indeed very few, and strangers in it. When they went from one nation to another, And from one kingdom to another people, He permitted no man to do them wrong; Yes, He reproved kings for their sakes. Saying, "Do not touch My anointed ones, And do My prophets no harm."*

How have we interpreted, *"Do not touch My anointed ones, And do My prophets no harm?"* The majority of today's Christians believe it means simply do not speak against your leadership. The verse has been interpreted Priestly instead of Kingly, making today's meaning a mere shadow of how David actually used it.

The core concept is God's willingness to **reprove kings** for His covenant partners! If **reproving kings** equals **terminating kings or**

rendering them powerless then our covenant has teeth. The church of the last fifty years has acted like a toothless tiger. When we look in Genesis 20 at what God said to Abimelech in verse 7, we see teeth in action: *"Now therefore, restore the man's wife; for he is a prophet, and he will pray for you and you shall live. But if you do not restore her, know that you shall surely die, you and all who are yours."* How did we ever interpret that as, Don't speak against leaders? This is the covenant-keeping God weighing back and willing to quickly cut off as many as it took to save Sarah. When David went to war, these Psalms declaring the covenant were continually sung before the Ark. You could not go to war with David and keep your head. David prayed judgment! Isn't it time the church found out that they have a covenant with God and He promises to "cut off" those who are destroying our future harvest? The covenant has teeth. Take a bite. Take a bite out of perversion. Take a bite out of abortion by praying covenant justice on legislative perpetrators. Will we rise up and actually be the end-time church without spot wrinkle or blemish? We presented Jesus as Savior to the Jews for a long time and many of them have said "No." It is time we presented them Jesus the Judge, Who is in fact the Messiah they have been looking for, for thousands of years. When Jewish people see Jesus the Judge in action, they will catapult into the Kingdom. It is time for biblical justice. It is time to pray like David prayed. It is time for the church to find her teeth! It is time to restore the fear of the Lord!

Through God there are exploits,
He wants you to fight.
When it comes to evil
Will you take a bite?

Jayne Houghton

Chapter 11

The Seven-fold Test

Before presenting prophetic interpretations of scripture as doctrine, it is always confirming to apply the seven-fold test of biblical continuity. First we should find the concept in Genesis in seed form. It should secondly appear somewhere within the Pentateuch; third, we should find it in the Psalms or Proverbs; fourth, the prophets should prophesy it; fifth, Jesus should teach it; sixth, it should be somewhere within the Acts of the early church; and seventh, we should find it in the Epistles. Applying the seven-fold test to prophetic teaching is like building forms and mixing cement so that once it is poured it forms a permanent foundation. When the Spirit and the Word unite we get spiritual cement upon which we can stand. A solid concrete biblical foundation is immovable. May every believer find spiritual cement that we know comes historically when God's Word and the Spirit unite.

1 John 3:18-21 speaks of a process by which our hearts have to be convinced before God that what we are doing is right. It says, *"My little children, let us not love in word or in tongue, but in deed and in truth. And by this we know that we are of the truth, and shall assure our hearts before Him. For if our heart condemns us, God is greater than our heart, and knows all things. Beloved, if our heart does not condemn us, we have confidence toward God."* Building confidence toward God is utterly essential to move in His justice.

Therefore, applying this seven-fold test is the process of persuading our heart and preparing to stand before the Lord declaring and decreeing justice by the Holy Spirit. Certain foundational questions such as, Does God expect us to move His Hand judicially, both to start or to stop judgment must be answered. My Bible thunders a "Yes" answer! If you discover the same biblical application, help me lift a generation of believers out of passivity and into the heat of the battle! Share this book with an equally committed friend! Rescue the next generation from passivity and prepare them for the power of the Spirit!

Genesis 18:16-19 declares God's purpose for establishing His covenant with man:

> *Then the men rose from there and looked toward Sodom, and Abraham went with them to send them on the way. And the LORD said, "Shall I hide from Abraham what I am doing, since Abraham shall surely become a great and mighty nation, and all the nations of the earth shall be blessed in him? For I have known him, in order that he may command his children and his household after him, that they keep the way of the LORD,* ***to do righteousness*** *and* ***justice****, that the LORD may bring to Abraham what He has spoken to him."*

Verse 19 clearly declares that God sought relationship with man and specifically covenant relationship with Abraham because He wanted an agent **to do justice**. Do you view yourself as an agent of God's justice? If not – why not? Abram's household kept the way of the Lord to do justice and judgment. The first Hebrew word describing what Abram was to do was **tsed-aw-kaw**, which is righteousness or justice. This word appears 421 times in the Hebrew Old Testament, with 296 of those instances translated as judgment. The second word was **mish-pawt**, the prophetic proclamation of a **shaw-fat**, a judge. Whenever a judge, such as Samuel, made a prophetic proclamation, it became a

mish-pawt, and in Samuel's case God did not allow any of his words to fall to the ground. The context of doing righteousness and justice or justice and judgment comes into view when a covenant culture departs from righteousness and embraces perversion. The outcry against Sodom demanded judgment. As nations adopt homosexuality, an outcry demands judgment!

Homosexual marriage can fill a land with iniquity so that the land has to be judged. Sin is very expensive! Filling a nation or a state with iniquity demands biblical justice and whether the people realize it or not, it will come. God gave Abram a voice in that judgment by covenantal relationship because he had family members that were in the designated area of destruction. In verses 25-26 Abraham began to fulfill his call outlined in verse 19. He said, *"Far be it from You to do such a thing as this, to slay the righteous with the wicked, so that the righteous should be as the wicked; far be it from You! Shall not the Judge of all the earth do (**mish-pawt**) right."* Abraham was pleading for justice, not to stop judgment.

If the church could make that transition, things would change. God sent an angel to insure justice. Lot was told by the angel to take his family and flee to the mountains. He pleaded for residing in a small city nearby, which he later abandoned for the mountains. Notice the power of Abraham's intercession in moving God's Hand over the issue of justice in what the angel said to Lot in Genesis 19:20-22, *"'See now, this city is near enough to flee to, and it is a little one; please let me escape there (is it not a little one?) and my soul shall live.' And he said to him, 'See, I have favored you concerning this thing also, in that I will not overthrow this city for which you have spoken. Hurry, escape there. **For I cannot do anything until you arrive there.**' Therefore the name of the city was called Zoar."* Abraham's intercession locked up the destruction of Sodom and Gomorrah until Lot entered the city of Zoar. Once Lot entered the city of Zoar divine justice fell on Sodom and Gomorrah.

Divine justice is falling again. The question is, Will the church be actively involved covenantally, like Abram was? Abraham through covenant moved God's Hand to save Lot in the midst of catastrophic devastation. How can we save the remnant righteous in a region such as San Francisco? When cities, states, or nations consistently spit in God's face with what they champion, there is no way to stop the judgment, only gain the removal of our family and loved ones. If San Francisco and Berkeley deserve a 10.0 earthquake, will anyone recognize an 8.7 was God's mercy diminished only by intercession? Genesis 18:19 makes God's intent for man clear, *"For I have known him, in order that he may command his children and his household after him, that they keep the way of the LORD,* ***to do*** *righteousness and justice, that the LORD may bring to Abraham what He has spoken to him."* God established covenantal relationship with man expecting us **to do** justice. We do that in intercession. We have a standing offer to participate with God in starting and stopping judgment! A growing number of ministers are teaching all judgment fell on Jesus and God is not judging today. That is a stunning denial of Revelation where Jesus begins judging the church and moves to the world. The Apostle Paul in the first few verses of 1 Corinthians 6 made clear the believer's assignment in judging the world and angels. Why would Paul deliver such an admonition to the church if it were not true? Jesus Christ is the same today as He was in the Old Testament. Jesus has not changed! Our access to redemption has changed from the law to a relationship with the Savior. The Savior is also the Judge of all the earth and He still judges those who choose to yield to the flesh.

Jesus Christ is the same yesterday, today, and forever! He judges sin and there will be some overthrown cities before history concludes! Leviticus 20 declares the creation cries for a cleansing as it fills with iniquity. The land upon which San Francisco and Berkeley are built has been crying for a cleansing for a long time – Thy Kingdom come, Thy will be done! Mercy is manifested in withheld judgment but it **will** come! The truth of divine justice has passed the first of the seven-fold tests: It was found in Genesis. Secondly, it must be found in the Pentateuch.

In the Pentateuch, Numbers 16 records the incident where Moses is challenged by Korah, Dathan, and Abiram and 250 leaders of the congregation. The complaint in Numbers 16:3 is a direct challenge to the leadership of Moses and Aaron, *"They gathered together against Moses and Aaron, and said to them, 'You take too much upon yourselves, for all the congregation is holy, every one of them, and the LORD is among them. Why then do you exalt yourselves above the congregation of the LORD?"* Verses 12-14 shed further light on the issue when they state,

> *And Moses sent to call Dathan and Abiram the sons of Eliab, but they said, "We will not come up! Is it a small thing that you have brought us up out of a land flowing with milk and honey, to kill us in the wilderness, that you should keep acting like a prince over us? Moreover you have not brought us into a land flowing with milk and honey, nor given us inheritance of fields and vineyards. Will you put out the eyes of these men? We will not come up!"*

Korah, Dathan, and Abiram and 250 leaders were all gathered together against Moses and Aaron at the door of the tabernacle of meeting. Moses warned the congregation to separate themselves from Korah, Dathan, and Abiram for justice sake because if they did not they would participate in their judgment. Verses 28-32 demonstrate God's Hand moving at Moses' words. Verses 33-35 record finishing the judicial act,

> *So they and all those with them went down alive into the pit; the earth closed over them, and they perished from among the congregation. Then all Israel who were around them fled at their cry, for they said, "Lest the earth swallow us up also!" And a fire came out from the LORD and consumed the two hundred and fifty men who were offering incense.*

The leaders could not stand in the fire they called down. Moses moved the Hand of God for justice as recorded in the Pentateuch.

Thirdly, can we find this principle of divine justice in the Psalms or Proverbs? Psalm 3 and Psalm 143 have to be taken together because they were both composed as David was fleeing from Absalom, his son. Psalm 3;1,2 says, *"LORD, how they have increased who trouble me! Many are they who rise up against me. Many are they who say of me, 'There is no help for him in God.'"* In the first two verses of Psalm 3 David marvels at how many people have joined Absalom and wonders how it could have happened. But the answer to how it happened is in 2 Samuel 15 and it is an issue of perverted justice, almost like the spirit of radical Islam. 2 Samuel 15:2-6 states:

> *Now Absalom would rise early and stand beside the way to the gate. So it was, whenever anyone who had a lawsuit came to the king for a decision, that Absalom would call to him and say, "What city are you from?" And he would say, "Your servant is from such and such a tribe of Israel." Then Absalom would say to him, "Look, your case is good and right; but there is no deputy of the king to hear you." Moreover Absalom would say, "Oh, that I were made judge in the land, and everyone who has any suit or cause would come to me; then I would give him justice." And so it was, whenever anyone came near him to*

bow down to him, that he would put out his hand and take him and kiss him. In this manner Absalom acted toward all Israel who came to the king for judgment. So Absalom stole the hearts of the men of Israel.

Absalom stole the hearts of the men of Israel by promising skewed justice. In verse 4 Absalom declared if he were made a **shaw-fat** Judge then he would give **tsaw-dak**, the root word for righteous judgment or justice, or the ability to make right according to God's moral standard, consequently to vindicate. However, when we go down to verse 6 we are told, *"In this manner Absalom acted toward all Israel who came to the king for **mish-pawt**/judgment. So Absalom stole the hearts of the men of Israel."* What apparently inflamed Absalom was David showing mercy to Amnon when his sister Tamar was raped. We do not know from the text about any penalties that David imposed on the perpetrator except that scripture says, in 2 Samuel 13:21, *"But when King David heard of all these things, he was very angry."* It may be that David understood the penalty for his own transgression was beginning to move its way through the family and the best way to pastor it was mercy, mercy, mercy. Perhaps if he had followed God's model with mercy for restoration but penalty for sin, the outcome may have changed. When the text is silent, everything else is speculation. We do know that David found himself in the unusual position of having to demand covenantal justice before the Throne on his own son who had stolen the kingdom. Absalom as described in scripture, appears to be a politician offering/promising every group exactly what they wanted to hear.

In Psalm 3, after hearing the declarations of false righteousness by Absalom's followers, David proclaims before the Throne in verses 3-4, *"But You, O LORD, are a shield for me, My glory and the One who lifts up my head. I cried to the LORD with my voice, And He heard me from His holy hill."* Verses 5-6 declare the power of the covenant, *"I lay down and slept; I awoke, for the LORD sustained me. I will not be afraid of ten thousands of people Who have set themselves against me all around."* Finally in verses 7-8 David declares covenant justice on the enemy, *"Arise, O LORD; Save me, O my God! For You have struck all my enemies on the cheekbone; You have broken the teeth of the ungodly. Salvation belongs to the LORD. Your blessing is upon Your people. Selah."* Possibly when David had more time to think about what had transpired he could discern cause and effect. The rebellion attracted the leading prophetic voice in the land. David had to respond to the defection of his very best friend and counselor who was the oracle of God in the capital in those days, named Ahithophel.

This betrayal was perhaps more painful than any other, at least we deduce that from David's words as he prays for biblical justice. Psalm 55:4-11 states:

> *"My heart is severely pained within me, And the terrors of death have fallen upon me. Fearfulness and trembling have come upon me, And horror has overwhelmed me." And I said, "Oh, that I had wings like a dove! For then I would fly away and be at rest. Indeed, I would wander far off, And remain in the wilderness. Selah. I would hasten my escape From the windy storm and tempest." Destroy, O Lord, and divide their tongues, For I have seen violence and strife in the city. Day and night they go around it on its walls; Iniquity and trouble are also in the midst of it. Destruction is in its midst; Deceit and guile do not depart from its streets.*

David brings before God the agony of his situation and then declares the general spiritual decline and debauchery that has taken over in Jerusalem. He knows the path. He knows that the end of the path that has been chosen by Absalom is judgment, and destruction, and he proclaims it. In a way he is asking for mercy for the people of the city and destruction on the perpetrators. This is called covenant vengeance or covenant justice. He gets more specific in verses 12-14, *"For it is not an enemy who reproaches me; Then I could bear it. Nor is it one who hates me who has magnified himself against me; Then I could hide from him. But it was you, a man my equal, my companion and my acquaintance. We took sweet counsel together, And walked to the house of God in the throng."* This is specifically spoken about Ahithophel, his best friend, his chief advisor, a man whose prophetic anointing was parallel to his. They worshipped together, they walked together, they prophesied together, they were soul mates in the spirit. But suddenly his best friend is now his chief enemy which happened because of the offense of David taking Bathsheba whose father was Eliam, whose father was Ahithophel. Bathsheba was Ahithophel's granddaughter.

It appears that Ahithophel blamed David for the calamity and shame that came upon the family. For Ahithophel, David's immoral betrayal was unforgiveable. The problem was that with God it was not. It was forgivable and God had given David a covenant of Sure Mercy spoken through Nathan the prophet upon which he stood. True repentance allowed God to redeem the failure by turning it into a strength. From this union came Solomon. This sin was never again found in David's life. God forgave him and from a position of righteousness he could stand upon the covenant and declare in Psalm 55:15-16, *"Let death seize them; Let them go down alive into hell, For wickedness is in their dwellings and among them. As for me, I will call upon God, And the LORD shall save me."* David's prophetic declaration for covenant justice was heard. Verses 17-21 continue in his declaration for covenant justice against Ahithophel and every companion of Absalom:

Evening and morning and at noon I will pray and cry aloud, And He shall hear my voice. He has redeemed my soul in peace from the battle which was against me, For there were many against me. God will hear, and afflict them, Even He who abides from of old. Because they do not change, Therefore they do not fear God. He has put forth his hands against those who were at peace with him; He has broken his covenant. The words of his mouth were smoother than butter, But war was in his heart; His words were softer than oil, Yet they were drawn swords. Cast your burden on the Lord, And He will sustain you; He shall not permit the righteous to be moved. But You , O God shall bring them down to the pit of destruction; Bloodthirsty and deceitful men shall not live out half their days; By I will trust in You.

David voices intercession in verses 22-23 declaring the full measure of covenant justice in utter complete victory. This was obviously an extended war for David and while it may have transpired over a few months' time, nevertheless his plea for covenant justice was a day and night issue until it was manifested. The Psalms witness to our ability to move God's Hand for justice!

Number four in the seven-fold test is, Did the Prophets preach it? In Isaiah 36-37 we find Israel under assault from the Assyrians and the leader of the Assyrian army comes to Jerusalem to deliver a letter demanding surrender. In verses 16-22 of chapter 36 he instructs:

Do not listen to Hezekiah; for thus says the king of Assyria: "Make peace with me by a present and come out to me; and every one of you eat from his own vine and every one from his own fig tree, and every one of you drink the waters of his own cistern; until I come and take you away to a land like your own land, a land of grain and new wine, a land of bread and vineyards. Beware lest Hezekiah persuade you, saying, 'The LORD will deliver us.' Has any one of the gods of the nations delivered its land from the hand of the king of Assyria? Where are the gods of Hamath and Arpad? Where are the gods of Sepharvaim? Indeed, have they delivered Samaria from my hand? Who among all the gods of these lands have delivered their countries from my hand, that the LORD should deliver Jerusalem from my hand?" But they held their peace and answered him not a word; for the king's commandment was, "Do not answer him.'" Then Eliakim the son of Hilkiah, who was over the household, Shebna the scribe, and Joah the son of Asaph, the recorder, came to Hezekiah with their clothes torn, and told him the words of the Rabshakeh.

Hezekiah took the letter into intercession. Does God promise to kill and destroy the enemy in covenant? The answer is unequivocally "Yes" if He can ever find anybody who will stand on the covenant and call it down. Isaiah 37:14-20 tells us Hezekiah's covenantal response to the letter promising destruction from the king of Assyria:

And Hezekiah received the letter from the hand of the messengers, and read it; and Hezekiah went up to the house of the LORD, and spread it before the LORD. Then Hezekiah prayed to the LORD, saying: "O LORD of hosts, God of Israel, the One who dwells between the cherubim, You are God, You alone, of all the kingdoms of the earth. You have made heaven and earth. Incline Your ear, O LORD, and hear; open Your eyes, O LORD, and see; and hear all the words of Sennacherib, who has sent to reproach the living God. Truly, LORD, the kings of Assyria have laid waste all the nations and their lands, and have cast their gods into the fire; for they were not gods, but the work of men's hands – wood and stone. Therefore they have destroyed them. Now therefore, O LORD our God, save us from his hand, that all the kingdoms of the earth may know that You are the LORD, You alone."

At the end of Hezekiah's prayer, Isaiah was summoned by the Lord with a declaration and given a prophetic word. Verse 21 makes it clear that God's response spoken by Isaiah is coming as a direct result of the prayer-action King Hezekiah took. The question is simple, Have you as a covenant believer ever taken this action? Most people would say "No" because this is Old Covenant and I am a New Covenant believer, but as we will see in Luke 18 Jesus taught us we could pray this. The question is, Have we? Unfortunately for the majority of the people in the church the answer to that question is probably "No." The condition of our nation reflects a probable "No." Verse 21 states, *"Then Isaiah the son of Amoz sent to Hezekiah, saying, 'Thus says the LORD God of Israel, "Because you have prayed to Me* ***against*** *Sennacherib king of Assyria, this is the word which the LORD has spoken concerning him:"'"* Verses 33-36 document an answer to a judicial prayer:

Therefore thus says the LORD concerning the king of Assyria: "He shall not come into this city, Nor shoot an arrow there, Nor come before it with shield, Nor build a siege mound against it. By the way that he came, By the same shall he return; And he shall not come into this city, Says the LORD. For I will defend this city, to save it For My own sake and for My servant David's sake." Then the angel of the LORD went out, and killed in the camp of the Assyrians one hundred and eighty-five thousand; and when people arose early in the morning, there were the corpses – all dead.

God's response to Hezekiah's intercession was quick, short, and to the point. Hezekiah simply voiced a demand for covenant justice. God sent an angel and the next day 185,000 were dead! Verses 37-38 declare, *"So Sennacherib king of Assyria departed and went away, returned home, and remained at Nineveh. Now it came to pass, as he was worshiping in the house of Nisroch his god, that Adrammelech and Sharezer his sons struck him down with the sword; and they escaped into the land of Ararat. Then Esarhaddon his son reigned in his place."* The question is, Does God expect us to move His hand in covenant justice? How can anyone read the prophets and think anything else except the lie of the enemy which is "That is just Old Testament"? That is why we have a seven-fold test for prophetic doctrine, the last three coming from the New Testament.

Did Jesus teach it? Luke 18 is a parable Jesus taught but the point is crystal clear. Verses 1-5 state:

> *Then He spoke a parable to them, that men always ought to pray and not lose heart, saying: "There was in a certain city a judge who did not fear God nor regard man. Now there was a widow in that city; and she came to him, saying, 'Avenge me of my adversary.' And he would not for a while; but afterward he said within himself, 'Though I do not fear God nor regard man, yet because this widow troubles me I will avenge her, lest by her continual coming she weary me.'"*

The Complete Word Study Dictionary of the New Testament defines **ek-dik-eh-o** as "at the hand of." This Greek word for "*avenge*" means, 'to execute justice, defend one's cause, maintain one's right or avenge the blood on or at the hand of.' Jesus encourages us to put a demand on God for covenant justice. In verses 6-8a, He says, *"Then the Lord said, 'Hear what the unjust judge said. And shall God not avenge His own elect who cry out day and night to Him, though He bears long with them? I tell you that He will avenge them speedily...'"* In verses 6-8a the

Greek word translated *"avenge"* is **ek-dik-ay-sis**. This word primarily means execution of right justice. The concept is repaying harm for harm on the basis of what is rightly deserved. It is the meting out of justice or doing justice to all parties. God promises to do justice for His elect, proving the covenant has not changed in this dimension. The New Covenant is every bit as good as the four preceding Theocratic Covenants in the Old Testament. The New Covenant stands in lock step with them on the issue of covenant justice. Finally, in this account Jesus issues the challenge of Luke 18:8b, *"...Nevertheless, when the Son of Man comes, will He really find faith on the earth?"* The definite article is used in the Greek meaning will He really find "this" kind of faith on the earth or the kind that demands covenant justice. That is a direct challenge to the Christians that wind up the age. When Jesus returns will He find the kind of faith that Abraham walked in, David walked in, Hezekiah walked in, and generation after generation of believers had available? Will we allow a religious spirit echoing, "That's just Old Testament" to steal our covenant right to justice? Thank God the early church stood their ground, and I trust when Jesus returns He will find those in the earth who demand an administrative decision for justice. It is available at the Throne if we will act on it! Jesus taught judicial access.

Can we find examples of divine justice in Acts? Do we find the early church in intercession and God's Hand of justice moving? We certainly find justice in Acts chapter 5, but there is no record of intercession moving God's Hand to dispose of Ananias and Sapphira! We have to wait for that until Acts chapter 12:1-2, *"Now about that time Herod the king stretched out his hand to harass some from the church. Then he killed James the brother of John with the sword."* Herod killed James and intended to do the same to Peter. But the church began to pray. Their prayer had two manifestations. Number 1, an angel came and released Peter. Number 2, possibly the same angel visited Herod and the principle of justice that Abraham experienced was initiated, "As you touch My people I will touch you." As Herod touched James, God touched Herod. Verses 21-23 state, *"So on a set day Herod, arrayed in royal apparel, sat on his throne and gave an oration to them. And the people kept shouting, 'The voice of a god and not a man!' Then immediately an angel of the Lord struck him, because he didn't give glory to God. And he was eaten by worms and died."* Herod died the most painful death known to man. I cannot say, after reading Acts, that the intercession or declaration of the church does not move God's Hand to justice, because in the very next chapter Paul brought blindness on a false prophet and so persuaded the politician and gained entrance into the region. Acts 13:8-12 states:

> *But Elymas the sorcerer (for so his name is translated) withstood them, seeking to turn the proconsul away from the faith. Then Saul, who also is called Paul, filled with the Holy Spirit, looked intently at him and said, "O full of all deceit and all fraud, you son of the devil, you enemy of all righteousness, will you not cease perverting the straight ways of the Lord? And now, indeed, the hand of the Lord is upon you, and you shall be blind, not seeing the sun for a time." And immediately a dark mist fell on him, and he went around seeking someone to lead him by the hand. Then the proconsul believed, when he saw what had been done, being astonished at the teaching of the Lord.*

Paul understood covenant. He was an Old Testament scholar. Paul lived in the New Testament. Although it had not yet been written, Paul acted like the Old Testament covenant still worked. When Jesus said He did not come to do away with the law or the prophets, apparently Paul believed Him! Jesus confirmed the New Covenant in His Blood guaranteeing previous covenant commitments. His Blood guarantees access to covenant justice. Praying for or against your enemies has to be **led by the Spirit**!

Perhaps we have had the wrong slant on praying for our enemies or perhaps we have just been blind to justice. Paul understood the difference between Priestly justice, praying for the enemies' salvation, and Kingly justice, praying for their removal. Apparently he allowed the Spirit to lead him. What a novel concept. May it gain favor among today's saints!

The final manifestation of divine justice in the New Testament needs to be seen in the Epistles. Where in the Epistles do we find anybody asking God for justice on their enemy instead of salvation? The most evident place for that would be one of the leading pastoral Epistles such as in 1 Timothy chapter 1, verses 18-20, where Paul is exhorting Timothy to walk in such a way as to keep a good conscience before the Lord, which is necessary to finish the race. He reminds him of two men who have not, and the consequences, *"This charge I commit to you, son Timothy, according to the prophecies previously made concerning you, that by them you may wage the good warfare, having faith and a good conscience, which some having rejected, concerning the faith have suffered shipwreck, of whom are Hymenaeus and Alexander, whom I delivered to Satan that they may learn not to blaspheme."* Paul's concept of justice included destruction! Does ours, or are we so Priestly we cannot do what Paul did in Acts 13 by blinding the false prophet?

In 2 Timothy 4, we find the second step of this ongoing warfare between Paul and an unrepentant Alexander. Verses 14-15 state, *"Alexander the coppersmith did me much harm. May the Lord repay him according to his works. You also must beware of him, for he has greatly resisted our words."* A Greek word describing God's principle for covenant justice is **ax-ee-os**, a weight and measure term. **Ax-ee-os** from

God's perspective is, 'As you have touched My people I will touch you.' That is precisely what Paul prays when he declares, *"May the Lord repay him according to his works."* Paul's prayer is against Alexander, not for Him. Has tradition robbed us of truth? What Paul prayed is a covenant justice declaration against a specific individual mentioned by name. It is not a prayer for salvation. It is an undeniable prayer for justice uttered by the Apostle Paul. Why are we afraid to go there? It is obvious that Paul went there, being led by the Holy Spirit all the way. Our problem is that religion has denied us this dimension of covenant, and nations are paying the price. It is time the church stood in the Throne Room and declared God's covenant.

God's storehouse of wisdom
Will guide you in prayer,
But without His direction
Don't venture there!

Jayne Houghton

Chapter 12

Pattern for Praying Covenant Justice

The Septuagint, the Vulgate, the Ethiopic, and the Arabic texts all declare Psalm 143 was composed upon Absalom's rebellion. Psalm 143 is a brilliant pattern prayer for executing covenant justice. Verses 1-2 state, *"Hear my prayer, O LORD, Give ear to my supplications! In Your faithfulness answer me, And in Your righteousness. Do not enter into judgment with Your servant, For in Your sight no one living is righteous."* From a New Testament perspective we would state, no one living in Your sight has done it all right. Now that is a brilliant thing to pray when you are getting ready to ask God for judgment. There is full recognition that when it comes to the issue of judgment, "Please don't enter into judgment with Your servant because the only place I can stand is a place of mercy and grace." An enemy who has abandoned mercy and grace has entered a path of destruction. He switches gears in verses 3-6, *"For the enemy has persecuted my soul; He has crushed my life to the ground; He has made me dwell in darkness, Like those who have long been dead. Therefore my spirit is overwhelmed within me; My heart within me is distressed. I remember the days of old; I meditate on all Your works; I muse on the work of Your hands. I spread out my hands to You; My soul longs for You like a thirsty land. Selah."* David's intercession and his stand on covenant justice is remarkable in this

Psalm, and if there was ever a blueprint for praying covenant justice it is Psalm 143.

In verse 12 he gives the ultimate plea for justice, *"In Your mercy cut off my enemies, And destroy all those who afflict my soul; For I am Your servant."* David invoked his covenant. God heard and answered. Jesus bought and paid for the Covenant of Sure Mercy being extended to every New Testament believer. We can almost hear David musing, "It is a covenant right, God? I did not dream up this Covenant of Sure Mercy but You did. You offered it to me and I said 'Yes.' Now perform it." This invocation of the covenant almost reminds us of what David prayed when he first received the Covenant of Sure Mercy in 2 Samuel 7:25, *"And now, O LORD God, the word which You have spoken concerning Your servant and concerning his house, establish it forever and do as You have said."* "God, You said it. It was Your idea. Now it is time to perform it. I'm calling it forth." In Psalm 143, David called for covenant justice according to God's righteous standard. His prayer was, in effect, "Let the axe fall now and let the enemy be removed." This is "picture perfect" Kingly justice executed through intercession, a biblical model that can be imitated today. The original recipient of the covenant demonstrates biblical implementation. David presents the principle that through covenant we can move God's Hand for justice. Absalom did not get one spear in his heart, nor did he get two, he got three – one for each member of the covenant-keeping Trinity! God is the God of justice. The God Who said to Abram, "The reason I've known you is so that you can do justice," is the same God who knew David. God elevated David in Acts 13 as an example for us whose heart we should imitate. Do we have a heart for war like David? Mercy and justice to David meant God moved to destroy his enemy! Are we demanding justice like David did?

Psalm 143 records David fleeing from Jerusalem, because **Absalom** had taken the throne. His intercession turned judicial. David ended this Psalm with a prayer demanding covenant mercy manifest in the death and destruction of the enemy. He prayed in verse 12: *"In Your mercy cut off..."* The **Hebrew** word translated *"cut off"* is **psaw-math.** It means to extirpate or utterly destroy, while the Hebrew word for *"destroy"* is **aw-bad,** which means to perish, die, or be exterminated. It is a Hebrew hiphel perfect verb meaning to destroy, to put to death, or bring divine judgment on *"...all those who afflict my soul; For I am Your servant."* David understood the Kingly application of covenant mercy. We have only understood Priestly mercy. When we think of covenant mercy we only think of one application and that is compassionate-mercy to every individual. David thought of covenant mercy in terms of mercy to the nation meaning God's destruction of the enemy. David understood that mercy had a cutting edge that was judgment unto utter destruction. Moses understood that and that is why after emerging from splitting the Red Sea in Exodus 15:13 we read: *"You in Your mercy have led forth The people whom You have redeemed; You have guided them in Your strength To Your holy habitation."* It was God's mercy that killed the entire Egyptian army – mercy to the Israelites meant death to the Egyptians.

Mercy to America means bankruptcy to certain media corporations. It would be God's mercy to America if He killed every terrorist cell that is intent on torturing and killing Christians and innocents. Mercy of this magnitude seems to primarily come as a heart-cry from only those who are perishing. David's heart-cry came under threat of Absalom's sword. Moses' heart-cry came under threat of Pharaoh's sword through the Egyptian army. Will the church cry under the Supreme Court's sword? Will we cry under the sword of pro-homosexual legislation? If the Spirit leads, will we cry against those who legislated it? When a legislator or judge declares any minister who preaches Romans 1 as guilty of discrimination, then at the Spirit's direction the weight of Romans 1 must be prayed against those individuals.

If you are thinking, I could never pray that, you are experiencing the fruit of tradition which nullifies God's Word! The church needs to be available to pray over every offending judge and politician bent on defiling and destroying the land!

Tradition makes the Word of God "of none effect." If our "turn-the-other-cheek" tradition prevents us from praying as David did, we could easily lose the nation. Please do not say: "I cannot pray that way. I could not ask God to destroy somebody. I am afraid that I am not qualified." David undoubtedly had the same issues, because at the time of losing his throne to Absalom, he had already been through the Bathsheba incident suffering the greatest moral failure of his life. Let God redeem your failure by learning to appropriate David's Covenant of Sure Mercy that Jesus guaranteed. (See book: *The Sure Mercies of David*). David prayed covenantally without guilt. He prayed a pattern we should consider following. Psalm 143 should be our personal failure Twelve-Step recovery plan. Psalm 143:1 says: ***"****Hear my prayer, O LORD, Give ear to my supplications! In Your faithfulness answer me, And in Your righteousness."* David begins his intercession by declaring God's faithfulness and righteousness because he knows the foundation of God's Throne are pillars of justice and righteousness and covenant guarantees access with faithfulness demanding corresponding action!

Verse two states, ***"****Do not enter into judgment with Your servant, For in Your sight no one living has done it all right****"*** (paraphrase). In verse 1 David declared "Who God is" and contrasts in verse 2 who man is. David masterfully compares God and man emphasizing man's simple nature and multiple shortcomings. Covenant relationship allows us to approach God, identify the enemy, and demand intervention. Romans 5:17 promises all *"...who receive the... gift of righteousness will reign in* *life through the One, Jesus Christ."* Jesus gave us His righteousness and we have to choose to put that on. When we choose to put on the righteousness of Christ, we can confidently pray, *"Do not enter into judgment with Your servant, O LORD, for no one in Your sight is without sin."* We could all agree with that. We are simply asking God not to enter into judgment with us individually because we stand **in Christ**. We received mercy individually by faith through repentance because Jesus **cut off** our sin. Psalms 143 is so brilliant in its relational progression, it had to be authored by the Holy Spirit!

After reminding God that all men are just flesh and asking for personal mercy, David switches gears by focusing on all the transgressions of the enemy. He says in verse 3: *"For the enemy has persecuted my soul; He has crushed my life to the ground; He has made me dwell in darkness, Like those who have long been dead."*

David moves from, "Do not judge Your servant, O LORD for all have sinned" into, "Look what the enemy has done to the heart of the church. The enemy is so vile that his darkness has been spread over all the land. It is so bad, so deep, so gross that in many places, the atmosphere is like those who have long been dead! Such is the perversion and abomination that has been spread throughout the nation." Seeker-sensitive Christianity has captured significant numbers in today's church. Profiteering preachers have plastered God's people with untempered mortar by accepting what He condemns. David painted a picture of just how successful the enemy had been in filling the land with iniquity. Talk about knowing how to persuade God by articulating your point of view – David was a master! Let the anointing that was on David now come to the church for praying our covenant and moving God's Hand! Let God's Hand move in the church first to destroy every untempered piece of plaster wherever it has been applied. According to Ezekiel 13:9-15:

My hand will be against the prophets who envision futility and who divine lies; they shall not be in the assembly of My people, nor be written in the record of the house of Israel, nor shall they enter into the land of Israel. Then you shall know that I am the Lord God. Because, indeed, because they have seduced My people, saying, "Peace!" when there is no peace – and one builds a boundary wall, and they plaster it with untempered mortar – say to those who plaster it with untempered mortar, that it will fall. There will be flooding rain, and you, O great hailstones, shall fall; and a stormy wind shall tear it down. Surely, when the wall has fallen, will it not be said to you, "Where is the mortar with which you plastered it?" Therefore thus says the Lord GOD: "I will cause a stormy wind to break forth in My fury; and there shall be a flooding rain in My anger, and great hailstones in fury to consume it. So I will break down the wall you have plastered with untempered mortar, and bring it down to the ground, so that its foundation will be uncovered; it will fall, and you shall be consumed in the midst of it. Then you shall know that I am the LORD. Thus will I accomplish My wrath on the wall and on those who have plastered it with untempered mortar; and I will say to you, 'The wall is no more, nor those who plastered it...'"

Ezekiel's word applies to today's church. David moved God's Hand to save his nation, Why can't we? Jesus cleansed the temple and told us to speak to the mountain and it would move! Jesus cursed the fig tree and it died, He then encouraged us to use our faith and do the same. God's exemplary shepherd of choice is David. David's heart is our model. Pray what David prayed! Cleansing the temple must start in the house of the Lord!

In Psalm 143:4 David says, "*Therefore my spirit is overwhelmed within me; My heart within me is distressed.*" Is your heart distressed by the condition of the church? Is your heart distressed when you see America's most successful pastors refuse to take a stand on abortion or homosexuality, claiming to be "uniters, not dividers?" Agree with Ezekiel – the untempered mortar cannot stand! David masterfully described the fruit of what the enemy had done and the inroads he had made in the land. He described the depth of darkness, because of the spiritual death that ruled and reigned everywhere and how it impacted God's church and God's servants. *"Therefore my spirit is overwhelmed within me; my heart within me is [utterly] distressed."* "God, I am overwhelmed. There is nowhere to go. There is no way out. I need You. You are the only answer. Human strength won't do anything. Without You I am without hope. Help Lord!" What a masterful approach in the Throne-Room! David knew how to pray! Jesus killed a fig tree with a declaration. Apostate leaders should face the same fate. Temple cleansing is necessary! Try it – it is Bible!

Psalm 143:5 says: *"I remember the days of old; I meditate on all Your works; I muse on the work of Your hands. I spread out my hands to You."* "I don't have the strength. I cannot do it. I'm overwhelmed. God, You can do it. I remember days when You did it. I'm thinking about all those deliverances. I'm thinking about what You did in Egypt. I'm thinking about how Your great right Hand moved at the prophetic word of Elisha and You brought blindness on an entire army. I'm thinking about all You did with Moses and how You delivered the people. I'm spreading out my hands to You so that Your Hand can move again. Do for us what You did for Joshua!" What an approach to God and what a stand on the covenant! What a way to describe the bankruptcy of his condition, as opposed to the utter invincibility of God's position. David is setting the stage to move God's Hand! What stage are we setting? Through intercession, set the stage for the justice of God! The Jesus of Revelation is ready to demonstrate justice.

Psalm 143:7 says: *"Answer me speedily, O LORD; My spirit fails! Do not hide Your face from me, Lest I be like those who go down into the pit."* David started pulling on God's heart. "God, if You wait, it is all over. I don't have an eternity. I don't have much time. I don't live in the realm of eternity like You do. My spirit is about to fail. But You could answer me in the snap of Your fingers. If You don't hide Your face, then I'll walk out of this in victory. But if You do, I will be taken into the pit never again to rise. Is that really what You want? Do You want my demise? Do You want my death or do You want my lips to praise You? I'm in Your hands. You are the covenant-keeping King. What will You do?" David pleads a strong case for timely intervention. One key element of judicial prayer is timing. This base should always be covered!

Verse 8 states, *"Cause me to hear Your lovingkindness in the morning, For in You do I trust; Cause me to know the way in which I should walk, For I lift up my soul to You."* David makes it clear to God, "I want to hear You every morning. I want You every day of my life. It is in You that I trust and in Your covenant I trust because You are the covenant-keeping God. You keep covenant to a thousand generations, therefore I will lift up my soul to You. God, I trust You. You are trustworthy." The brilliance of David's presentation in his intercession is almost beyond words. He is praying as if his very life depends on it! In fact, it does! How are we praying? Psalm 143:9 says: *"Deliver me, O LORD, from my enemies; In You I take shelter."* Here again we find a heartfelt plea. "Deliver me, the enemy is out there. My life hangs in the balance. My only shelter is in You." How would David pray for America? "God, if You don't come through, it is over. If You don't come through, we lose the nation. If You don't stand and fight for us, everything our forefathers spilled their blood for is gone from the earth and they connected You with the United States of America. IN YOU,

GOD, WE TRUST. Ride on the wings of the wind and come down. Take hold of every politician advancing the homosexual agenda against your church and let the fruit of their doings capture their own families first, until they have no seed left!" Would David have any reservation in moving God's Hand to utterly annihilate every evil agenda of our elite media or of Americans united for the "Separation of Church and State"? I believe if we would follow this pattern we would see the Hand of God move in such a dramatic way that the majority of people in the church would be stunned at what God does to the enemy. The God of Justice is ready to move for the church! All we have to do is follow David's lead in how to activate that covenant. Maintaining relationship with God through righteousness is a key. God did exactly what David asked!

Psalm 143:10 says: *"Teach me to do Your will, For You are my God; Your Spirit is good. Lead me in the land of uprightness."* "God, here I am. I'm teachable. I don't know it all. There is a whole lot that I have missed but I trust You to teach me. I trust You to get me there. You won't abandon me. Your Spirit is good. You know how to lead me out of this imminent death into utter deliverance. You know how to save the day and get the glory in the process so that everybody recognizes that **You** did it! Once again make **Your name glorious**. Once again hear the praises of the people who say, 'OUR FATHER DID IT!' Cleanse the land, remove those judges and legislators whose support of homosexual marriage fill our land with iniquity. Destroy those who refuse to turn – destroy them before their actions destroy our land."

Psalm 143:11 says: *"Revive me, O LORD, for Your name's sake! For Your righteousness' sake bring my soul out of trouble."* 'God, You gave me a Covenant of Sure Mercy – it wasn't my idea. Sure, I've blown it, but Your covenant of mercy says You would make my greatest mistakes a platform for the ultimate victory, and that my mistakes You would redeem and they would praise You. And I know You are going to do that and You can't do it when the enemy wins. You can't do it if we lose the nation. The only way to do it is to save the land.' What a brilliant progression of intercession. Did it work? Everyone who came against David in the rebellion died. It worked! David was delivered and his office restored!

This great crescendo of intercession ends in verse 12. David culminates his prayer with an appeal to the imprecatory side of the Covenant of Sure Mercy. He says, *"In Your mercy cut off my enemies, And destroy all those who afflict my soul; For I am Your servant."* David understood the difference between individual mercy and corporate mercy. Individual mercy saves us from our sin. Corporate mercy saves us from the enemy who is trying to destroy our land. If the church can first, understand the difference between individual and corporate mercy and second, pray accordingly, we may well see a visible Hand in the heavens coming upon those who refuse to turn. Tolerating evil destroys the land. The prayers of the saints should move God's Hand to destroy individual terrorist cells. Just as the early disciples moved God's Hand to destroy Herod, we should see the Hand of God coming on those who destroy Kingdom purposes. The intercession of the church can move God's Hand in our behalf! Isn't it time we offered a thanksgiving to God in the Davidic pattern outlined by Psalm 143? God is ready. Are we?

We see judges and leaders creating laws that protect sin and those same leaders supporting school curriculums that normalize or encourage sin. This creates a culture where the cup of iniquity fills so quickly that devastating judgment becomes necessary to cleanse the land. We see evidence of this fact in recent times. One example is, every year since one governor signed more pro-homosexual legislation than any other governor in history, his state has seen a billion dollars a year required for dealing with catastrophic fires. Leaders legislating sin deserve a Psalm 143:12 intercessory response from the church. When State Supreme Court Justices void the sanctity of marriage to protect homosexual marriage or spill innocent blood by protecting and underwriting abortion, Psalm 143:12 should be invoked by the entire church on every participating judge. Psalms 2:10-12 declares God's willingness to deal with contrary leaders during a season of harvest, *"So, rebel-kings, use your heads, Upstart-judges, learn your lesson: Worship God in adoring embrace, Celebrate in Trembling Awe. Kiss Messiah! Your very lives are in danger, you know, His anger is about to explode, but if you make a run for God-you won't regret it!"* (*The Message*). When there is no fear of God in the land only judgment will restore it. Covenant judgments are available and should be directed upon those who refuse to repent! Where are David's "mighty men" to save the land?

I flew many missions in Vietnam and this true story of a friend redeems every day of every year I spent there:

> *"If your God is real, prove it to me and I will let you go!" The harsh words of the police officer were directed at a Stieng tribal pastor from the highlands of Vietnam. "I don't speak enough Vietnamese to explain it to you," the pastor replied, praying quietly for wisdom as he gave his answer. "But if you die tonight, you will be sure to see God." The prison officer motioned in disgust for the guards to escort the pastor back to his cell. It was already late in the evening and he had no more patience for the questioning of this tribal man who could barely speak Vietnamese. He would continue it tomorrow and maybe his luck would turn and he could put an end to the explosion of Christianity among the Stieng tribe in the nearby hills. However the next morning, the officer never showed up for work. He had died during the night of unknown causes. His family and the local doctor were mystified. But the guards*

at the local police station remembered the words of the simple tribal pastor. From that time on, in March 1999, no police officers have dared to interfere with this Stieng pastor, and his church has been left to multiply in peace. When we access Jesus the Judge, the harvest can be reaped!

Let's activate the covenant
And follow David's lead.
Be clothed with justice...wisdom...truth
Preparing to succeed!

Jayne Houghton

Chapter 13

Arise Shine

Isaiah 60:1-5 prophesies a season of great harvest:

> *Arise, shine; For your light has come! And the glory of the LORD is risen upon you. For behold, the darkness shall cover the earth, And deep darkness the people; But the LORD will arise over you, And His glory will be seen upon you. The Gentiles shall come to your light, And kings to the brightness of your rising. Lift up your eyes all around, and see: They all gather together, they come to you; Your sons shall come from afar, And your daughters shall be nursed at your side. Then you shall see and become radiant, And your heart shall swell with joy; Because the abundance of the sea shall be turned to you, The wealth of the Gentiles shall come to you.*

The church is very familiar with the glory of the Lord that is promised for a mighty end-time harvest where people of all walks of life run to the church because of the glory they see in manifestation. Many moves of the Spirit have promised to result in the fulfillment of Isaiah 60:1-5 and yet we are still looking for the glory to wind up the age. It is possible that Isaiah 60:1-5 is a response to the church's heart-cry for justice that comes from the adverse cultural circumstances described in Isaiah 59:11b-21, during which "justice stands afar off." Context demands this consideration. If this is the case and it seems quite likely, then we have a key ingredient as to why previous moves of the Spirit have not continued. The persecution of the church coupled with massive injustice on a global scale contribute to filling a cup of iniquity. The intercessory heart-cries of the church access Throne-Room justice where God's Hand is moved by our prayers to accomplish justice. The adversity of Egypt prompted groaning too deep for words, and that groaning culminated in Moses' judicial anointing. So too, the innocent blood of 50 million aborted children cries for justice, and we trust a judicial anointing is at hand!

The promised fullness of Isaiah 60 is most likely the fruit of Isaiah 59:11b-16. The problem is identified as one where justice is turned back because righteousness is not embraced. As government continues to spit in God's face, He is preparing the church to voice His heart as He shines forth justice! God had an answer and in that answer He was coming as an intercessor to establish justice and our access to it. We know from previous chapters that has been accomplished. Verses 17-19 say:

> *For He put on righteousness as a breastplate, And a helmet of salvation on His head; He put on the garments of vengeance for clothing, And was clad with zeal as a cloak. According to their deeds, accordingly He will repay, Fury to His adversaries, Recompense to His enemies; The coastlands He will fully repay, So shall they fear The name of the LORD from the west, And His glory from the rising of the sun; When the enemy comes in like a flood, The Spirit of the LORD will lift up a standard against him.*

Paul taught Ephesians 6 from this passage. A good way to check our interpretation of Isaiah 59 and 60 is to look at how Paul interpreted it in Ephesians chapter 6. A broad look at the book of Ephesians traces the theme of fullness in every chapter. The theme of fullness runs from

Genesis through Revelation.

The theme of Ephesians is the fullness of Christ:

Chapter 1:22-23 says, *"And He put all things under His feet, and gave Him to be head over all things to the church, which is His body, the **fullness of Him** who fills all in all."*

Chapter 2:19-22 says, *"Now, therefore, you are no longer strangers and foreigners, but fellow citizens with the saints and members of the household of God, having been built on the foundation of the apostles and prophets, Jesus Christ Himself being the chief cornerstone, in whom the whole building, being joined together, grows into the holy temple in the Lord, in whom you also are being built together for a **habitation of God** in the Spirit."*

Chapter 3:17-19 says, *"...that Christ may dwell in your hearts through faith; that you, being rooted and grounded in love, may be able to comprehend with all the saints what is the width and length and depth and height – to know the love of Christ which passes knowledge; that you may be filled with all the **fullness of God**."*

Chapter 4:11-13 says, *"And He Himself gave some to be apostles, some prophets, some evangelists, and some pastors and teachers, for the equipping of the saints for the work of ministry, for the edifying of the body of Christ, till we all come to the unity of the faith and the knowledge of the Son of God, to a perfect man, to the measure of the stature of the **fullness of Christ**..."*

Chapter 5:18 says, *"And do not be drunk with wine, in which is dissipation; but be **filled with the Spirit**..."*

Chapter 6:10-12 says, *"Finally, my brethren, be strong in the Lord and in the power of His might. Put on the **whole armor of God**, that you may be able to stand against the wiles of the devil. For we do not wrestle against flesh and blood, but against principalities, against powers, against the rulers of the darkness of this age, against spiritual* *hosts of wickedness in the heavenly places."*

It is obvious that the fullness of Christ is the promise of Ephesians, accomplished, bought, and paid for by the Lord Jesus Christ. The question is how would Paul apply what he taught in Ephesians out of Isaiah 59? The answer to that question is in the context of Isaiah 59. Verses 13-18a tells us:

> *In transgressing and lying against the LORD, And departing from our God, Speaking oppression and revolt, Conceiving and uttering from the heart words of falsehood. Justice is turned back, And righteousness stands afar off; For truth is fallen in the street, And equity cannot enter. So truth fails, And he who departs from evil makes himself a prey. Then the LORD saw it, and it displeased Him That there was no justice. He saw that there was no man, And wondered that there was no intercessor; Therefore His own arm brought salvation for Him; And His own righteousness, it sustained Him. For He put on righteousness as a breastplate, And a helmet of salvation on His head; He put on the garments of vengeance for clothing, And was clad with zeal as a cloak. According to their deeds, accordingly He will repay, Fury to His adversaries, Recompense to His enemies...*

Paul understood the armor to be our access to Throne-Room justice. He taught Ephesians from the context of bringing forth divine justice. Verses 19-20 describe intercession first and foremost to be for the church that they may have utterance, persevere, and come into the full measure God has for them.

Paul was in the midst of great injustice himself because he was writing this book from his first Roman imprisonment between A.D. 60 and 62. He was expecting divine justice to get out of jail. We know from Philippians that he expected to visit again the churches. Paul knew

Throne-Room justice. He had accessed it many times and he was reminding the Ephesians, even while in prison. Isaiah 59 pictures access to Throne-Room justice based on intercession. For Paul, Throne-Room justice ruled even over Caesar. In Ephesians 3:10-12 Paul outlined the purpose for the church as, *"...to the intent that now the manifold wisdom of God might be made known by the church to the principalities and powers in the heavenly places, according to the eternal purpose which He accomplished in Christ Jesus our Lord, in whom we have boldness and access with confidence through faith in Him."* Our access with confidence through faith in Him interpreted in Ephesians 6 is Throne-Room justice. It is through accessing Throne-Room justice that we demonstrate or teach principalities and powers that they do not rule our nation or any part of our government. Principalities should not rule the state Supreme Court. They should not rule a state through a demonized, deceived governor. They should not rule a state through deceived justices. We have an obligation to access Throne-Room justice, demand mercy for the land, and trust God's Hand to cut off those individuals. By moving in this realm we teach principalities and powers that God not His enemies rule in the affairs of men.

Where are the warriors who must put a demand on God's covenant and bring the glory or lift the standard against evil that Jesus guaranteed in Isaiah 59? We are told that when the enemy comes in, like a flood the Spirit of the Lord will lift up a standard against him. That standard that Paul proclaimed in Ephesians 3 is to be a church that teaches principalities and powers by demonstration that they do not rule through deceived politicians. We know Paul practiced what he believed because when he faced a demonized deceived prophet, in Acts 13, attempting to keep him from a region, he accessed Throne-Room justice and proclaimed the Hand of the Lord upon that individual and that he would be blind for a season. The politician *"...believed when he saw..." the* doctrine of the Lord. Where is the doctrine of the Lord in the church today? It has, to a large part, been lost. It has been lost to "turn-the-other-cheek" Christianity taken out of context. It is time for the restoration. Isaiah 59 finishes with a very strong covenant promise in verse 21, *"'As for Me,' says the LORD, 'this is My covenant with them: My Spirit who is upon you, and My words which I have put in your mouth, shall not depart from your mouth, nor from the mouth of your descendants, nor from the mouth of your descendants' descendants,' says the LORD, 'from this time and forevermore.'"* God promised that the same covenant, guaranteeing the flow of His Spirit to Isaiah would anoint the words of our mouth in any situation we face.

When Jesus was teaching the Twelve and getting ready to release them for the first time in Matthew 10:16-20, He warned them saying:

> *Behold, I send you out as sheep in the midst of wolves. Therefore be wise as serpents and harmless as doves. But beware of men, for they will deliver you up to councils and scourge you in their synagogues. And you will be brought before governors and kings for My sake, as a testimony to them and to the Gentiles. But when they deliver you up, do not worry about how or what you should speak. For it will be given to you in that hour what you should speak; for it is not you who speak, but the Spirit of your Father who speaks in you.*

Isn't it interesting that Jesus taught the Twelve to be at peace? He said that even in the very hour of great adversity the Spirit of their Father would rise with an answer. Where did Jesus get that assurance? He did not have the New Testament. Where did that come from? The answer has to be found somewhere in Isaiah 59. Isaiah 59 expresses God's commitment to justice. The promise is that intercessory cries will be heard and answered. Intercessory cries will result in demonstrations.

As we approach the end of the age, greater and greater cumulative injustice rises. The prophets agree in promising the "last days" church double of what we find in Acts. God promises to double the anointing that the first generation church experienced. There is an Isaiah 60 in our future and it may well be nearly here! It is possible that the manifestation of Isaiah 60 is the fruit of the church rising and demanding justice as chapter 59 promises. If the church raises the standard against evil, expect the promised glory to manifest.

The Spirit of the Lord will rise upon God's people as a barrier or standard that will be lifted up. The Redeemer will come to Zion and God's covenant promises a manifestation of the Spirit to stop evil when it threatens a promised national harvest. Psalm 2 declares that Jesus died for nations. The Holy Spirit comes upon us with an anointing to bring forth His justice. This continues until the end of the age. If we were to view Isaiah 59 as teaching that the intercessory heart-cry for justice brings an anointing that displaces darkness, then we might prepare a generation to embrace the birthing of Isaiah 60. Justice is available at every level – justice judicially, justice financially, justice morally, justice educationally, justice in every dimension. Perhaps the pathway to maintaining the glory and not forfeiting it is cultivating the heart-cry for justice in a church that sustains it. Maybe God is waiting for us. Perhaps our problem has been our theology. What would it look like if we were to apply the heart-cry for justice to the promise of Isaiah 60:5? How would we form an intercessory outcry? We could start by charting the generational thefts of the enemy. We have a biblical right to demand justice for every theft in every generation for which we are aware.

Jesus proclaimed in John 10:10 that, *"The thief does not come except to steal, and to kill, and to destroy,"* and he has done that financially for generations. It appears that the enemy has looked at generations of righteous people and engineered circumstances where offenses have cut them out of wills. There has been a demonic assault to disinherit the righteous. The cumulative effect of excessive loss is to render God's people incapable of doing what is in their heart in the last days. Thievery by the spirit of mammon over generations has culminated in a reservoir of injustice in the realm of the Spirit that looks like a mighty dam holding back great provision. The one word written on the door is JUSTICE. I saw a picture of it in the Spirit! On top of the dam were a number of levers waiting to be opened that would release what had been dammed up but those levers were only opened by the heart-cries of people for justice. In Isaiah 61 God promises the restoration of the desolations of many generations. There must rise an intercessory outcry over the injustice of what has been stolen generationally that will culminate in an Isaiah 60 manifestation covenantally.

Financial justice is accessible through intercession which must be embraced and consistently offered before the Throne. It may be that the heart-cry for justice over what has been taken culminates in overflowing abundance. A wealth transfer is promised to the church. Fulfillment and release could be titled "The Anointing to Spoil." Whenever a thief was caught in scripture, he had to restore a multiple of what was taken. Restoration varied according to what was stolen. As early as Exodus 22:1 we are told, *"If a man steals an ox or a sheep, and slaughters it or sells it, he shall restore five oxen for an ox and four sheep for a sheep."* Proverbs 6:30-31 states, *"People do not despise a thief If he steals to satisfy himself when he is starving. Yet when he is found, he must restore sevenfold; He may have to give up all the substance of his house."* One constant emerges in the study of biblical justice financially: (1) There is always a multiple that must be restored based on what has been stolen. (2) A heart-cry for justice must rise by the Spirit in intercession. (3) Justice dictates thieves lose, saints win in a transfer. (4) A believer must covenantally demand Throne-Room justice. *"Shall not the God of all the earth do right?"* (See CD Series, "The Anointing to Spoil.")

Adversity tills the soil from which a heart-cry for justice can be heard!

God even takes responsibility in Joel 2 for four levels of devastation that come to His people for character development. Joel 2:23-27 says:

> *Be glad then, you children of Zion, And rejoice in the LORD your God; For He has given you the former rain faithfully, And He will cause the rain to come down for you – The former rain, And the latter rain in the first month. The threshing floors shall be full of wheat, And the vats shall overflow with new wine and oil. So I will restore to you the years that the swarming locust has eaten, The crawling locust, The consuming locust, And the chewing locust, My great army which I sent among you. You shall eat in plenty and be satisfied, And praise the name of the LORD your God, Who has dealt wondrously* [**paw-law**] *with you; And My people shall never be put to shame. Then you shall know that I am in the midst of Israel, And that I am the LORD your God And there is no other. My people shall never be put to shame.*

There is a definite promise of provision for an end-time harvest that culminates in a double anointing when the cumulative cup fills. Decades of devastating circumstances cry out. When the righteous demand a great judicial end-time balancing of the scales, covenant is initiated. Verse 26 could hardly be any more obvious about the provision promised and its declaration of a divine **paw-law**. When God deals wondrously with us, things change quickly and dramatically! The concept embodied in this Hebrew word dates to the angels who visited Sarah when she laughed about the possibility of having a son at her advanced age. The angels' response to Sarah's laughter at the impossibility of her situation is recorded in Genesis 18:13-14, *"And the LORD said to Abraham, 'Why did Sarah laugh, saying, "Shall I surely bear a child, since I am old?" Is anything too* ***paw-law****/hard for the LORD? At the appointed time I will return to you, according to the time of life, and Sarah shall have a son.'"* We really do not want to find ourselves in Sarah's place having to deny our unbelief, but it is obvious that when God does something wondrous, He does it according to a specific time of life, whether that be individual or generational. There is a prophetic cry for justice that should result in a generational restoration of what has been stolen for the purpose of a great end-time harvest. Scripture is clear and it seems to indicate in Isaiah 59 and 60 that what instigates this outpouring is a heart-cry from the church and a demand for covenant justice! Isn't it time we did some computations concerning what has been stolen generationally and craft a prayer of restoration and demand covenant justice before the Throne? The proof is in the pudding. Do it! Do it consistently! And see what God does!

Twenty years ago the Lord began to deal with me about the issue of how He paid for and built the very first church buildings in scripture and asked me if I knew, and I, of course, said "No," and He said, "Find out." I discovered that the tabernacle of Moses was built from the freewill offerings that people gave from what they collected when they spoiled Egypt. The temple of Solomon was built out of the spoil that came from the anointing that was on David and therefore by covenant transferred to his mighty men. In both cases what was given for the building projects came from "spoiling the enemy." After tracing this thread prophetically from the Old Covenant to the New, the biblical principle of the "Anointing to Spoil" passed the seven-fold test of prophetic doctrine. The Lord directed me to teach and impart this anointing to businessmen believing, based on prophesies in Isaiah, that God would use businesses in the end-time to spoil for His prophetic purposes. The initial response to the business seminars I did, where the whole purpose was to lay hands on men and women and impart the anointing to spoil, was in most cases an avalanche of adversity. I told the Lord, "Ministry should bless the church and not diminish it!" God's response to me was simply, "It's a covenantal anointing and as long as the spirit of mammon governs the heart this anointing will act like covenant judgment, but when the person is delivered it will bring covenant blessing."

As I began to reread the foundational scriptures, I discovered something I had not seen initially over the seven year period that God unfolded the "Anointing to Spoil." I noticed that the "Anointing to Spoil" was an issue of Divine Justice and therefore an executable judgment. Exodus 12:36 says, *"And the LORD had given the people favor in the sight of the Egyptians, so that they granted them what they requested. Thus they plundered the Egyptians."* "Plundering the Egyptians" was the fruit of judgment that was released in verse 12, *"For I will pass through the land of Egypt on that night, and will strike all the firstborn in the land of Egypt, both man and beast; and against all the gods of Egypt I will execute judgment: I am the LORD."*

The reason God executed judgment on Egypt was cumulative generational fullness of iniquity. Eighty years previously Pharaoh had ordered the killing of every Jewish male in an attempt to destroy the deliverer by having him drowned in the Nile. Four hundred years of captivity filled the cup. Conditions progressively worsened for the Israelites. The last 80 years were the worst. God destroyed and drowned the remaining strength of Egypt on the way out, after He struck all the firstborn. Egypt received multiple judgments based on all they had done, the next to the last one being spoiling by the Israelites. I realized that the anointing to spoil was, in fact, a manifestation of Divine Justice and a judgment that had to be executed.

The primary spirit competing for man's worship is mammon. Every individual must choose to either serve God or mammon: many of today's ministers are serving both because of how they manipulate for money!

Jesus executed a judgment on the enemy according to Matthew chapter 12 and taught that the fruit of executing that judgment was an anointing to spoil available to the church. Matthew 12:28-30 states, *"But if I cast out demons by the Spirit of God, surely the kingdom of God has come upon you. Or else how can one enter a strong man's house and plunder his goods, unless he first binds the strong man? And then he will plunder his house. He who is not with Me is against Me, and he who does not gather with Me scatters abroad."* Jesus spent three days and three nights in the belly of the earth and when *"He arose in a mighty triumph o'er His foes"* He made justice available to every one of us and guaranteed ultimate victory. Verses 28-30 are in the same context of the declaration of Matthew 12:18-21 about Isaiah's prophecy concerning Jesus taking justice to victory. There is a heart-cry for covenantal justice that releases an anointing to spoil. Apparently it comes no other way. When the church grows to the place of putting a demand in the Throne-Room for covenant justice over all that has been taken, we should see some dramatic changes if we do not lose heart and continue in patience, consistently putting a demand on covenant.

The resources of earth belong to the church for a great harvest. Even James got a glimpse of it in chapter 5 verses 1-9 where he stated:

> *Come now, you rich, weep and howl for your miseries that are coming upon you! Your riches are corrupted, and your garments are moth-eaten. Your gold and silver are corroded, and their corrosion will be a witness against you and will eat your flesh like fire. You have heaped up treasures in the last days. Indeed the wages of the laborers who*

mowed your fields, which you kept back by fraud, cry out; and the cries of the reapers have reached the ears of the Lord of Sabaoth. You have lived on the earth in pleasure and luxury; you have fattened your hearts as in a day of slaughter. You have condemned, you have murdered the just; he does not resist you. Therefore be patient, brethren, until the coming of the Lord. See how the farmer waits for the precious fruit of the earth, waiting patiently for it until it receives the early and latter rain. You also be patient. Establish your hearts, for the coming of the Lord is at hand. Do not grumble against one another, brethren, lest you be condemned. Behold, the Judge is standing at the door!

The problem with most of us in reading James chapter 5 is we get hung up on verse 7 and the issue of *"...the coming of the Lord"* and our thinking defaults to rapture. If we have to wait to receive financial justice until the rapture, where could we spend it? How can we spend earth's money in heaven? We only need justice on this issue if we are still here and trying to bring in a harvest. The promise is that the Lord will come with an anointing and execute justice for us. Jesus is the Judge Who is standing at the door. He is waiting for the church to walk in harmony with each other and to declare covenant justice. This passage seems to say that when we put a demand on justice the Judge is ready to bring it to pass. Surely we can position ourselves to put a demand on financial covenantal justice. Perhaps God is waiting on us.

A harvest is coming,
So rise up and shine.
Take back the landscape
That's rightfully Mine!

Jayne Houghton

Chapter 14

How did Jesus Judge?

It is amazing that many believers today are convinced they are not to judge anything, which, as a strategy from hell, seems to have been quite effective. Apparently the enemy has done a good job of using scripture to silence the church and render it utterly passive in the face of his assaults on nation after nation and the historical freedom of Christians, especially in America.

One of the great rebukes to the church in Thyatira, in Revelation 2:20, is *"Nevertheless I have a few things against you, because you allow..."* The Greek word for *"allow"* is **eh-ah-o** which means 'to tolerate, to refuse to restrain or to be passive in the face of.' Why is the church passive in the face of secularism? Why is it passive in the face of homosexual marriage? Why is it now passive over the issue of abortion? Jesus pronounced a number of judgments, some of which should shake us to our very core. Perhaps most amazing is Matthew 7:21-23, *"Not everyone who says to Me, 'Lord, Lord,' shall enter the kingdom of heaven, but he who does the will of My Father in heaven. Many will say to Me in that day, 'Lord, Lord, have we not prophesied in Your name, cast out demons in Your name, and done many wonders in Your name?' And then I will declare to them, 'I never knew you; depart from Me, you who practice lawlessness!'"* How is it possible to prophesy in the name of the Lord, to cast out demons, to do wonders, and then have Jesus say to you, after moving in the power of the Holy Spirit,

"...depart from Me, you who practice lawlessness... I never knew you." Every Spirit-filled Christian should look at this passage and say, "God, show me what that means. Where is the application, how is it possible to move in the power of the Holy Spirit and come to the place that Jesus declared many occupy? Save us from such a place."

Paul, in Philippians 3:17-19, sheds some light on this path to paralysis, *"Brethren, join in following my example, and note those who so walk, as you have us for a pattern. For many walk, of whom I have told you often, and now tell you even weeping, that they are the enemies of the cross of Christ: whose end is destruction, whose god is their belly, and whose glory is in their shame – who set their mind on earthly things."* How we use God-given faith may be one key. Paul declares it possible to use faith to comfort ourselves instead of using faith to embrace the cross and submit to the direction of the Holy Spirit.

It is intriguing to postulate the possibility of using our faith to build a great ministry, and only at the end of our life to have God declare that the very ministry we are the proudest of is the very thing of which we should be the most ashamed. Imagine building a church of 50,000 people but building it on principles that God considers rebellious. Ezekiel 13:9-15 describe exactly such ministries:

> *My hand will be against the prophets who envision futility and who divine lies; they shall not be in the assembly of My people, nor be written in the record of the house of Israel, nor shall they enter into the land of Israel. Then you shall know that I am the Lord GOD. Because indeed, because they have seduced My people, saying, "Peace!" when there is no peace – and one builds a boundary wall, and they plaster it with untempered mortar – say to those who plaster it with untempered mortar, that it will fall. There will be flooding rain, and you, O great hailstones, shall fall; and a stormy wind shall tear it down. Surely,*

when the wall has fallen, will it not be said to you, "Where is the mortar with which you plastered it?" Therefore thus says the Lord GOD: "I will cause a stormy wind to break forth in My fury; and there shall be a flooding rain in My anger, and great hailstones in fury to consume it. So I will break down the wall you have plastered with untempered mortar, and bring it down to the ground, so that its foundation will be uncovered; it will fall, and you shall be consumed in the midst of it. Then you shall know that I am the LORD. Thus will I accomplish My wrath on the wall and on those who have plastered it with untempered mortar; and I will say to you, "The wall is no more, nor those who plastered it."'

Recently I was going to minister in the Lone Star state of Texas. A violent weather front approaching Dallas with dangerous wind shears delayed our flight several hours. After rushing to the airport for an early morning flight, I sat and sat wondering if I could make my connection and if the scheduled church meeting that night would be cancelled. I decided to redeem the time by opening my Bible to see if the Lord had anything to say. He began to speak about the consequences of priests and prophets who profane the Holy Covenant through manipulation for money. I began to tell the Lord I felt this was the very reason He had given the principles which became the book *Purifying the Altar.* My Bible fell open to Ezekiel 22:23-26. The Lord impressed me that a divine reckoning was coming to all who profaned His covenant. Church leaders who have a heart for Jesus are the most precious people in the world! Those intent on building something successful through compromising the truth and refusing to address sin profane the Covenant and will achieve their appointed reward. Jesus the Judge visited the church first!

Ezekiel describes a ministry that is built on only teaching covenantal blessing and refusing to address issues of sin. Those who refuse to teach the difference between the holy and the profane are courting disaster. Ministries who refuse to say anything that will drop the biblical plumbline in their culture for fear of alienating people and losing their contributions have defiled altars. That is why Ezekiel 22:25 says, *"...they have taken treasure and precious things; they have made many widows in her midst."* Ezekiel said the fruit of refusing to address sin and iniquity in a land is that the land gets filled with iniquity and the people lose it. The military can no longer defend it. As fullness grows, adversaries abound. Nations find themselves in ill-advised wars that produce many widows. The real issue is not necessarily the spiritual condition of a nation's political leaders but a refusal by the church to deal with sin in the land, and God holds church leadership responsible, whether it be pastor, prophet, or priest. Priests and princes are held accountable and the root issue is the love of money.

Another contributing factor from Philippians 2:19-24 says:

> *But I trust in the Lord Jesus to send Timothy to you shortly, that I also may be encouraged when I know your state. For I have no one like-minded, who will sincerely care for your state.* ***For all seek their own****, not the things which are of Christ Jesus. But you know his proven character, that as a son with his father he served with me in the gospel. Therefore I hope to send him at once, as soon as I see how it goes with me. But I trust in the Lord that I myself shall also come shortly.*

Paul says, *"...all seek their own..."* Ezekiel told us exactly what to expect when priests and princes bow to money. Jesus said there are two spirits that compete for man's worship – God and money. The choices we make in how we use our faith, whether for self or others will determine which one is worshipped and what Jesus says to us on

Judgment Day.

Hebrews 11 gives us examples of men who used their faith on their flesh, obeyed God, embraced the cross and walked out God's purpose. Abraham, *"the father of all those who believe,"* is one great example. He had to use his faith to leave his country, his kindred, and his culture, and march out to the destination that was only a promise, with no idea of where it was. Because he used his faith and embraced the cross and walked out God's purpose, he became *"the father of all those who believe"* and our example.

Joseph is another example who was sold into slavery, then thrown into a prison and falsely accused. Moses' parents had to put him on the water, in faith. Moses, in faith, said "No" to being a son to Pharaoh's daughter and said "Yes" to his Hebrew heritage that cost him everything for 40 years. He used his faith to embrace the plan of God and paid the price in the process. Paul is speaking to the issue that Jesus has promised to judge and Hebrews gives us a multitude of examples. Jesus has already told us that "*men*" are going to be told to "*depart... I never knew you*" and the issue is how we use our faith.

Names of men who have used their faith to build large ministries through knowingly, selectively, cunningly neglecting to preach the cross come to mind. They refuse to preach the cross because the cross does not sell!

The end-time church is going to have a choice in how they use their faith. We need to start preparing a generation to use their faith to stand up in the face of deadly opposition and declare the Word of the Lord – even to the cost of our own lives. Jesus pronounced some spectacular judgments in the form of "woes" and we should understand them!

Matthew 23 is the transitional chapter where Jesus defines the fullness of iniquity that has encompassed the religious system and pronounces eight judicial "woes" which mark the end of the reign of the Pharisees and the religious system they perverted. The church age begins and Jesus as Judge of all the earth initiates justice. Jesus defined the foundation for their judgment in verses 2b-12:

> *"...The scribes and the Pharisees sit in Moses' seat. Therefore whatever they tell you to observe that observe and do, but do not do according to their works; for they say, and do not do. For they bind heavy burdens, hard to bear, and lay them on men's shoulders; but they themselves will not move them with one of their fingers. But all their works they do to be seen by men. They make their phylacteries broad and enlarge the borders of their garments. They love the best places at feasts, the best seats in the synagogues, greetings in the marketplaces, and to be called by men, 'Rabbi, Rabbi.' But you, do not be called 'Rabbi'; for One is your Teacher, the Christ, and you are all brethren. Do not call anyone on earth your father; for One is your Father, He who is in heaven. And do not be called teachers; for One is your Teacher, the Christ. But he who is greatest among you shall be your servant. And whoever exalts himself will be abased, and he who humbles himself will be exalted."*

Jesus described a money-based religious system that was political to the core. It was based on manipulation and had long lost its servanthood motivation. This system became completely divorced from the God they claimed to represent and therefore had to be judged and destroyed. Forty years later in A.D. 70, the temple and city were annihilated. In verse 13 Jesus outlined "woe" number 1, *"But woe to you, scribes and Pharisees, hypocrites! For you shut up the kingdom of heaven against men; for you neither go in yourselves, nor do you allow those who are entering to go in."*

How do preachers shut up the Kingdom of heaven and make it hard to enter? One of the ways is that they demonize people who teach and preach something they disagree with. The terms "kingdom of heaven" and "kingdom of God" are used interchangeably in the New Testament for the rule and reign of Christ in any situation. In Matthew 19:22-24 Jesus was speaking to the rich young ruler and said, *"But when the young man heard that saying, he went away sorrowful, for he had great possessions. Then Jesus said to His disciples, 'Assuredly, I say to you that it is hard for a rich man to enter the kingdom of heaven. And again I say to you, it is easier for a camel to go through the eye of a needle than for a rich man to enter the kingdom of God."*

This passage makes it clear that the "kingdom of heaven" and the "kingdom of God" are phrases that Jesus used interchangeably for the rule and reign of God in an individual's life when they were willing to completely and totally submit to Him. Jesus invited followers to a life of service. The Pharisees were kingdom-builders but the kingdom built was their own, ultimately earning the assessment, *"Depart from Me you that work iniquity, I never knew you."*

In Matthew 23:13, Jesus pronounced the first "woe" against those who hinder people from coming into the full measure of God's truth in order to preserve their own ministry. The second "woe" follows very closely on the heels of the first one, and proclaims a devastating judgment on a counterfeit religious system. Matthew 23:14 says, *"Woe to you, scribes and Pharisees, hypocrites! For you devour widows' houses, and for a pretense make long prayers. Therefore you will receive greater condemnation.'"* It is one thing to hinder people from coming into the truth. It is another to pretend spirituality by supposed gifts of healings or miracles to advance one's ministry and raise funds. How we use our faith in ministry will either line up with the Master's or be judged. Using our faith to promote self earns a "woe"! Using our faith to promote the church earns a blessing. Who are the ones today who make a pretense of church but never actually bring forth the truth and teach the people the difference between the holy and the profane?

Ezekiel was a prophet in captivity who knew well the fruit of a religious system that would never confront sin but only preach the covenantal blessing. He knew the fruit of it because he lived in captivity with the people when the judgment came and they lost their nation. Every person who sowed into that seemingly good work lost everything they had because they were funding a bankrupt system full of pretense which refused to tell the whole truth. If Jesus were to go to church with us on Sunday, would He slap a "woe" on the front of our church based on the choices the leadership is making? Have they knowingly retreated from declaring the full truth in the hopes of attracting a few more people? Is the job of the church to attract a large crowd or to be salt? (See book: *Converts or Disciples*). Whenever a minister refuses to teach the people the difference between the pure and the impure, the holy and the profane, people giving to his ministry are impacted. Every dollar put into that altar takes each believer closer to spiritual bankruptcy because we become one with the altar where we sow. (See book: *Purifying the Altar*).

The third "woe" is in Matthew 23:15, *"Woe to you, scribes and Pharisees, hypocrites! For you travel land and sea to win one proselyte, and when he is won, you make him twice as much a son of hell as yourselves."* The third woe is pronounced against a religious system for reproducing itself. Every altar we sow into starts growing in us. When a minister chooses to compromise the Word in his ministry and conduct it in such a way as to only teach what is popular, majoring only on multiple blessing, then a false prophet is born. When a minister majors in healing, wealth transfer, or what most appeals to the flesh, then everyone they minister to becomes impacted by their compromise. The minister transfers that spirit to listeners and he becomes accountable to God for the disciples he makes and the spiritual reproduction that takes place due to the influence of that leader. For compromisers, getting the success they pursue could kill them! Jesus was very clear about His standard of discipleship in John 17. Verses 6-10 bring real clarity to the true principle of discipleship for both preacher and parishioner. Only one standard prepares people for entering eternity. In verses 6-7 we are told, *"I have manifested Your name to the men whom You have given Me out of the world. They were Yours, You gave them to Me, and they have kept Your word. Now they have known that all things which You have given Me are from You."* Jesus did not withhold anything necessary for character development that the Father gave Him for the disciples. He gave it to them as they were able to hear it and consequently they reproduced themselves in men that changed the world. Verse 8 is the centerpiece of Jesus' discipleship. It says, *"For I have given to them the words which You have given Me; and they have received them, and have known surely that I came forth from You; and they have believed that You sent Me."* Jesus did not withhold the hard things and many left as a result of His honesty. How many topics are not addressed on Sunday morning for fear of losing people? The Bible is very clear about sin. It is clear about homosexuality. It is clear about abortion. The Bible is very clear. When we choose not to preach or speak specific passages that make clear God's will, we qualify for "woe" number 3. Every minister and believer must choose to obey or hear, "Depart from Me you worker of iniquity, I never knew you!" Let us not qualify for "woe" number 3, but choose to give *everything* God has given us. Then in eternity we can rejoice in verses 9-10 which say, *"I pray for them. I do not pray for the world but for those whom You have given Me, for they are Yours. And all Mine are Yours, and Yours are Mine, and I am glorified in them."* Jesus said in verse 10, if we want to see the fruit of any ministry look at the people who are its disciples.

Is what you read here the **true** word of the Lord? An excellent test is to look at the fruit. Look at the people who read it – look at the people who believe it and watch how they act. If this book presents the **true** Word of the Lord, readers who sow the principles into their lives will become one with the truths and power will be imparted to them. When students of the Word believe it, their faith rises, and they become a standard in the earth by which others can be judged.

But if ministers preach exclusively "turn-the-other-cheek," "do-not-resist-evil," they may be danger of the "woe." Matthew 23:16-22 describes "woe" number 4;

> *Woe to you, blind guides, who say, "Whoever swears by the temple, it is nothing; but whoever swears by the gold of the temple, he is obliged to perform it." Fools and blind! For which is greater, the gold or the temple that sanctifies the gold? And "Whoever swears by the altar, it is nothing; but whoever swears by the gift that is on it, he is obliged to perform it." Fools and blind! For which is greater, the gift or the altar that sanctifies the gift? Therefore he who swears by the altar, swears by it and by all things on it. He who swears by the temple, swears by it and by Him who dwells in it. And he who swears by heaven, swears by the throne of God and by Him who sits on it.*

"Woe" number 4 is a two-edged sword. It is a rebuke for majoring on money rather than purity. For seven straight years in the early '80s the Lord began to deal with me about a prophetic truth that scripture calls, "the Anointing to Spoil," at the rate of one principle a year. There is an "Anointing to Spoil" appointed for an end-time generation. It is a judgment that has to be executed and therefore each individual who is called to walk in it has to be able to stand in the fire they call down.

Mixed-seed ministries disqualify themselves at every level. The ministers who prepare this generation have to be able to sanctify, set apart, and teach each individual to distinguish the difference between the holy and the profane, between pure ministry and mammon/money motivation. The inability to discern love of money earns us a "woe"! Avoiding this "woe" is the purpose of the book entitled *Purifying the Altar.* As believers, we must develop discernment to recognize those who manipulate for money. Assimilating the principles of *Purifying the Altar* will change your life!

"Woe" number 5 is in Matthew 23:23-24, *"Woe to you, scribes and Pharisees, hypocrites! For you pay tithe of mint and anise and cumin, and have neglected the weightier matters of the law: justice and mercy and faith. These you ought to have done, without leaving the others undone. Blind guides, who strain out a gnat and swallow a camel!"* Avoiding "woe" number 5 should not be that difficult because you are reading a book that is dedicated to discerning the difference between justice, mercy, and faith. As this truth takes root, you may have moments when you begin to look just like Jesus cleaning house in the temple.

The sixth "Woe" is in Matthew 23:25-26, *"Woe to you, scribes and Pharisees, hypocrites! For you cleanse the outside of the cup and dish, but inside they are full of extortion and self-indulgence. Blind Pharisee, first cleanse the inside of the cup and dish, that the outside of them may be clean also."* Woe number 6 goes directly to the refusal to be transparent and the pretense of trying to be something we are not. Not everyone who claims to be a Christian will pay the price to develop Christ-likeness. There is coming a day when we will readily be able to see the difference between those who were willing to have their heart dealt with and those who were not, and the difference will be the protection and power of the Holy Spirit in the last days. God is raising up an army and it is not an army of weasels. It is an army who can bring the justice of God right out of their lips because they have allowed the Spirit to deal with personal issues. Transparency is a qualification for this army and what you see is what you get! Consider that when choosing a church.

"Woe" number 7 is in verses 27-28, *"Woe to you, scribes and Pharisees, hypocrites! For you are like whitewashed tombs which indeed appear beautiful outwardly, but inside are full of dead men's bones and all uncleanness. Even so you also outwardly appear righteous to men, but inside you are full of hypocrisy and lawlessness."* "Woe" number 7 nails the facade of religion. Religion has a form of godliness but denies the power when applied. What does Christianity without the cross look like? Philippians 3:17-19 describes it, *"Brethren, join in following my example, and note those who so walk, as you have us for a pattern. For many walk, of whom I have told you often, and now tell you even weeping, that they are the enemies of the cross of Christ: whose end is destruction, whose god is their belly, and whose glory is in their shame – who set their mind on earthly things."* Paul said there are many people who never embrace the cross. They are not enemies of Christ but they just refuse to embrace the cross. They never learn to nail themselves on the cross, therefore 'self' continues to rule.

Instead of training self to serve, they allow self to rule. Paul said their *"...end is destruction, whose god is their belly, and whose glory is in their shame..."* Now imagine attending a very successful church where compromise to gain achievement is the founding philosophy. Eating at this altar means this attitude will grab ahold of you. As long as you camp out there, you will never learn to discern the difference between the holy and the profane! You suddenly face Jesus with the other members of the congregation as screaming infants demanding why the pastor never told you truth? By the time you should have eaten meat you could only digest milk. Was it your fault or the pastor's? As a leader, the thing that you count as your greatest success can easily become the source of your greatest shame. What is successful to man can be abomination to God. For those who really do not think Jesus would send anybody to hell because of what some misguided ministers preach, think again in light of this "woe." Where we go to church can leaven and defile us until we can make little progress for the Kingdom!

Matthew 26:20-25 states:

> *Now when evening had come, He sat down with the twelve. Now as they were eating, He said, "Assuredly I say to you, one of you will betray Me." And they were exceedingly sorrowful, and each of them began to say to Him, "Lord, is it I?" Then He answered and said, "He who dipped his hand with Me in the dish will betray Me. The Son of Man goes as it is written of Him, but woe to that man by whom the Son of Man is betrayed! It would have been good for that man if he had not been born." Then Judas, who was betraying Him, answered and said, "Rabbi, is it I?" He said to him, "You have said it."*

Jesus made it very clear to Judas he would have been better off to have never been born. Well, if that does not culminate in hell, I do not know what does. Everybody who knows the Bible account, knows how he died, and knows what was purchased with the money he received for betraying Jesus.

Is Jesus the Judge? Does He have any problem sending people to hell? Absolutely not! Does He pronounce judgment? After eight woes in Matthew 23, the last defining statement before articulating the judgment is verse 32, "*Fill up, then, the measure of your fathers' guilt.*" How is it that we only see Jesus as Savior and we really do not know Him as Judge? How can we represent the Judge of all the earth if we do not know Him as Judge? The very first thing that happened when Jesus died on the cross was a significant judgment. Matthew 27:50-51 states, *"Jesus, when He had cried out again with a loud voice, yielded up His spirit. And behold, the veil of the temple was torn in two from top to bottom; and the earth quaked, and the rocks were split..."* When the *"veil of the temple was torn in two,"* it revealed an Ark-less Holy of Holies. The holiest place of all in Judaism was empty. The religious system was spiritually bankrupt for all to see.

There was no Ark because Jeremiah had hidden it during the destruction of Jerusalem and the following captivity. Herod's temple had a Holy of Holies that was Ark-less. The Ark walked among them and they did not recognize Him. What a picture of a plumbline establishing justice! What is amazing is the disciples became the same kind of plumbline. When God called Abram, His promise was: How people treat you is how I treat them. Because of this covenant every believer is invited to qualify as a plumbline. We have not trained a generation in how to be a plumbline nor how to represent Jesus the Judge or stand in fire that needs to be called down. Nearly twenty-four months of preparation was required before I ever got to fly my first combat mission. It feels like the church desperately needs to be cleared for combat but is just entering Boot Camp. May the Lord speed us through flight school!

Let's major on purity,
Tell the truth straight.
Let's be a plumbline,
Not just a dead weight.

Jayne Houghton

Chapter 15

Using the Psalms to Declare Justice

When the early church called for justice, they relied on covenant promises often presented in the Psalms. In Acts 1:19-20 we're told concerning Judas, *"And it became known to all those dwelling in Jerusalem; so that field is called in their own language, Akel Dama, (that is, Field of Blood.) For it is written in the book of Psalms: 'Let his habitation be desolate, And let no one live in it'; and, 'Let another take his office.'"* Before the early church ever received the Holy Spirit, they dealt with the fruit of judgment. They saw the Hand of God on Judas, bowels gushing out justice! When it came time to fill Judas' position they quoted the Psalms declaring their fulfillment. Acts 1:20 refers to Psalm 69, a major imprecatory judicial Psalm, and says in verses 20-29:

> *Reproach has broken my heart, And I am full of heaviness; I looked for someone to take pity, but there was none; And for comforters, but I found none. They also gave me gall for my food, And for my thirst they gave me vinegar to drink. Let their table become a snare before them, And their well-being a trap. Let their eyes be darkened, so that they do not see; And make their loins shake continually. Pour out Your indignation upon them, And let Your wrathful anger take hold of them. Let their habitation be desolate; Let no one dwell in their tents. For*

> *they persecute him whom You have struck, And talk of the grief of those You have wounded. Add iniquity to their iniquity, And let them not come into Your righteousness. Let them be blotted out of the book of the living, And not be written with the righteous. But I am poor and sorrowful; Let Your salvation, O God, set me up on high.*

This is a declaration of justice.

It is obvious that both Jesus and the disciples were quite familiar with the imprecatory prayers in the Psalms and referred to them on a number of occasions. When Jesus was on the cross, He uttered words that came right out of the imprecatory Psalms. Psalm 22:1 states, *"My God, My God, why have You forsaken Me? Why are You so far from helping Me, And from the words of My groaning?"* Verses 14-18 state:

> *I am poured out like water, And all My bones are out of joint; My heart is like wax; It has melted within Me. My strength is dried up like a potsherd, And My tongue clings to My jaws; You have brought Me to the dust of death. For dogs have surrounded Me; The assembly of the wicked has enclosed Me. They pierced My hands and My feet; I can count all My bones. They look and stare at Me. They divide My garments among them, And for My clothing they cast lots.*

Verse 31 states, *"They will come and declare His righteousness to a people who will be born, That He has done this."* The Septuagint uses the same verb as Jesus uttered, *"It is finished."* We need to remember that Israel used the Psalms as a Prayer Book. The question is: Do we teach today's church to use the Psalms as a Prayer Book? The unfortunate answer is "rarely" or "only selectively." The church to its own hurt does not pray as David prayed. If Jesus used it – we can use it.

The next question should be how did Peter and the apostles use the

Psalms? For the answer to that question we look squarely at their writings. Matthew 16 reveals the encounter where Jesus elicited the disciples' response as to Who He really was. Peter had the right answer. He said in verse 16, *"You are the Christ, the Son of the living God."* Jesus blessed Peter for that and declared that on that rock of revelation He would build His church and the gates of Hell would not prevail against it. The interesting part is what transpired next. Jesus began to tell His disciples exactly what was going to happen to Him, He had to be killed and raised again the third day. This created a conflict for Peter because Peter knew the Messiah of the Psalms. Knowing the Messiah of the Psalms brought a very strong reaction from Peter. Matthew 16:22 states, *"Then Peter took Him aside and began to rebuke Him, saying, 'Far be it from You, Lord; this shall not happen to You!'"* Where did that come from? Peter's prophetic eschatology came directly from the Psalms.

The Messiah of the Psalms is the victorious Judge of all the earth, while the Suffering Servant had been hidden from their eyes. Jesus had to rebuke Peter and tell him he was an offense for trying to thwart the plan of salvation. This does not change the fact that Peter knew the Messiah of the Psalms. After the betrayal, the death, burial, and resurrection in John 20 we find Peter and the others determined to return to something stable, the business of fishing. In John 21:3 we are told, *"Simon Peter said to them, 'I am going fishing.' They said to him, 'We are going with you also.' They went out and immediately got into the boat, and that night they caught nothing."* Jesus had to intervene. He met them and told them which side of the boat to throw the net and their catch was overflowing with fish. Peter jumped into the water, having recognized the Lord, and swam to shore. Jesus had a dramatic encounter with Peter that ended by telling him that when he was young he went wherever he wanted, he walked where he wished, but when he was old he would stretch out his hands and another would gird him and carry him where he did not wish to go. Peter's final preparation came by the filling of the Holy Spirit.

In Acts 2 when the Holy Spirit came and they were accused of being drunk, Peter stood up and began to quote the prophet Joel followed by Psalm 16:8-11. He came to the final conclusion of the issue by quoting Psalm 110:1 in Acts 2:32-36:

> *This Jesus God has raised up, of which we are all witnesses. Therefore being exalted to the right hand of God, and having received from the Father the promise of the Holy Spirit, He poured out this which you now see and hear. For David did not ascend into the heavens, but he says himself: "The LORD said to my Lord, 'Sit at My right hand, Till I make Your enemies Your footstool.'" Therefore let all the house of Israel know assuredly that God has made this Jesus, whom you crucified, both Lord and Christ.*

Peter used Psalm 68:18 and Psalm 110:1 to describe being filled with the Holy Spirit. Psalm 110 is the most quoted Psalm in the New Testament and it is 100% about executing covenantal justice. Psalm 110 says:

> *The LORD said to my Lord, "Sit at My right hand, Till I make Your enemies Your footstool." The LORD shall send the rod of Your strength out of Zion. Rule in the midst of Your enemies! Your people shall be volunteers in the day of Your power; In the beauties of holiness, from the womb of the morning, You have the dew of Your youth. The LORD has sworn and will not relent, "You are a priest forever According to the order of Melchizedek." The Lord is at Your right hand; He shall execute*

> *kings in the day of His wrath. He shall judge among the nations, He shall fill the places with dead bodies, He shall execute the heads of many countries. He shall drink of the brook by the wayside; Therefore He shall lift up the head.*

Peter steadfastly held on to the Messiah of the Psalms as the Judge of all the earth. The Suffering Servant had been hidden from Israel and still is a mystery to most. Peter knew the Messiah, therefore he held on to the Judge of all the earth empowering the church. He proclaimed the Holy Spirit as the agent of the anointing of the Messiah of the Psalms and three chapters later, he proved it. Acts 5:1-5 says:

> *But a certain man named Ananias, with Sapphira his wife, sold a possession. And he kept back part of the proceeds, his wife also being aware of it, and brought a certain part and laid it at the apostles' feet. But Peter said, "Ananias, why has Satan filled your heart to lie to the Holy Spirit and keep back part of the price of the land for yourself? While it remained, was it not your own? And after it was sold, was it not in your own control? Why have you conceived this thing in your heart? You have not lied to men but to God." Then Ananias, hearing these words, fell down and breathed his last. So great fear came upon all those who heard these things.*

Peter prophetically perceived that the infilling of the Holy Spirit brought Jesus the Judge. The Messiah of the Psalms came to live among us and His authority is now resident with us. After Acts chapter 5 no one in his generation could doubt Peter's interpretation of scripture explaining the infilling of the Holy Spirit in Acts 2. It has taken years of tradition to lose what the early church birthed.

Nobody could doubt Peter believed exactly what he said in Acts 2. How is it that some of us who desire to see the church filled with the Holy Spirit at times neglect the Messiah of the Psalms that Peter and Paul proclaimed? Does Paul proclaim the Messiah of the Psalms? In Romans 11 Paul deals with the fullness of the harvest, by quoting Psalm 69:22-23 which says, *"Let their table become a snare before them, And their well-being a trap. Let their eyes be darkened, so that they do not see; And make their loins shake continually."* This imprecatory Psalm describes physical Israel's fate until the Gentile harvest is full. Can anybody doubt that the man who moved God's Hand in Acts 13 to bring blindness on the false prophet has any problem at all praying or using the imprecatory Psalms? The final chapter of Romans 16 refers to Psalm 110 when he says in verses 17-20:

> *Now I urge you, brethren, note those who cause divisions and offenses, contrary to the doctrine which you learned, and avoid them. For those who are such do not serve our Lord Jesus Christ, but their own belly, and by smooth words and flattering speech deceive the hearts of the simple. For your obedience has become known to all. Therefore I am glad on your behalf; but I want you to be wise in what is good, and simple concerning evil. And the God of peace will crush Satan under your feet shortly. The grace of our Lord Jesus Christ be with you. Amen.*

Paul believed the God of peace would crush Satan under his feet because he knew Psalm 110 and, like Peter, he believed the anointing of the Holy Spirit was present to manifest divine justice. How can we neglect so great a salvation?

The Eastern church believed that the book of Hebrews was written by the Apostle Paul. The Western church disagreed but said they had no idea who wrote it. If we were to consider the possibility of Hebrews being written by the Apostle Paul, we would have a plethora of usage of imprecatory Psalms. Hebrews 1:7-9 is particularly interesting in the light of how the chapter ends. *"And of the angels He says: 'Who makes His angels spirits And His ministers a flame of fire.' But to the Son He says: 'Your throne, O God, is forever and ever; A scepter of righteousness is the scepter of Your Kingdom. You have loved righteousness and hated lawlessness; Therefore God, Your God, has anointed You With the oil of gladness more than Your companions.'"* Verses 10-14 wind up the chapter with a declaration out of Psalm 110 which perfectly fits with Paul's theology:

> *And: "You, LORD, in the beginning laid the foundation of the earth, And the heavens are the work of Your hands; They will perish, but You remain; And they will all grow old like a garment; Like a cloak You will fold them up, And they will be changed. But You are the same, And Your years will not fail." But to which of the angels has He ever said: "Sit at My right hand, Till I make Your enemies your footstool"? Are they not all ministering spirits sent forth to minister for those who will inherit salvation?*

Paul knew Jesus the Judge and believed He was readily accessible. You do not declare blindness on a false prophet without knowing the Judge of all the earth!

Hebrews 10:11-14 states, *"And every priest stands ministering daily and offering repeatedly the same sacrifices, which can never take away sins. But this Man, after He had offered one sacrifice for sins forever, sat down at the right hand of God, from that time waiting till His enemies are made His footstool. For by one offering He has perfected forever those who are being sanctified."* It is obvious that the New Testament church understood the power of praying the Psalms. They were not afraid of stepping out and asking God to take someone out OR covenantally cut them off. They were not afraid to lay down their life or to move the Hand of the Lord on somebody for blindness to gain God's purpose. The early church believed that the Messiah was the Judge of all the earth and like Shadrach, Meshach, and Abed-Nego their attitude toward covenant promise was, Daniel 3:17-18, *"If that is the case, our God whom we serve is able to deliver us from the burning fiery furnace, and He will deliver us from your hand, O king. But if not, let it be known to you, O king, that we do not serve your gods, nor will we worship the gold image which you have set up."*

The Apostle John had a similar experience when immersed in boiling oil without harm. He could have added a footnote to Revelation 19:11, *"Then I saw heaven opened, and behold, a white horse. And He who sat on him was called Faithful and True, and in righteousness He judges and makes war."* His footnote would have said, "See the Acts of Peter and Paul." It is time we decided that we can participate with Jesus, Peter, Paul, Mordecai Ham, and countless others in judging and making war. Why should misguided politicians fill our land with iniquity, aborting the promised harvest? God's purpose for the church is to teach by demonstration that God rules, not principalities and powers through deceived politicians and leaders. Jesus made every believer an agent of divine justice. It is time we earned our badge!

Will you tolerate evil
Which brings on destruction?
Or are you volunteering
To arise with God's unction?

Jayne Houghton

Chapter 16

Rules of Engagement

Pinnacle prayers for justice arise from the Davidic Psalms. Every believer should spend at least six months immersing themselves in the Psalms of David as preparation for prayer. A heart for war will surely emerge so that we can take our place in the rebuilt Tabernacle of David. Many of the Psalms that David wrote had the specific purpose of being prayed before the Ark. The demands for covenantal justice were not just David's words but they were actually God's words. In my experience, only immersion in the Davidic Psalms can deliver the church from the tradition that shapes how we pray and how we act. American culture cultivates acceptance of diverse views. The fruit of this tolerance is passivity in the face of evil. We have a generation of believers who seem willing to accept what God hates and judges. Surveys indicate nine out of ten Christians may not have a Christian-world view. David was not passive. He was a warrior. Warriors are not always nice. David prayed this in Psalm 55:13-15, *"But it was you, a man my equal, My companion and my acquaintance. We took sweet counsel together, And walked to the house of God in the throng. Let death seize them; Let them go down alive into hell, For wickedness is in their dwellings and among them."* It is hard for most New Testament believers to consider praying verse 15, *"Let death seize them; Let them go down alive into hell, For wickedness is in their dwellings and among them."* Yet it was a divinely inspired Holy Spirit-originated prayer. David was in a situation where his kingdom had unjustly been taken from him. How much have misguided politicians and judges taken from the church? Repossessing it was David's covenantal biblical obligation. We should respond as he did toward every judgment or decision that counters biblical principles. We have a right to covenantally pray as David prayed. We must understand that those words in the Psalms were actually God's Words given by the Holy Spirit. They were given to us as an example of how to war! These things were written for our training upon whom the ends of the world have come! We have every right to pray those words and expect the same results!

David said himself about the Psalms, in 2 Samuel 23:1-3, *"Thus says David the son of Jesse; Thus says the man raised up on high, The anointed of the God of Jacob, And the sweet psalmist of Israel: 'The Spirit of the LORD spoke by me, And His word was on my tongue.' The God of Israel said, The Rock of Israel spoke to me: 'He who rules over men must be just, Ruling in the fear of God.'"* Why is the church afraid to pray what the Holy Spirit put on the lips of David in his situation when we find ourselves in a parallel place? Ignorance is no longer an excuse. Covenant is covenant to a thousand generations. Jesus bought and paid for the Covenant of Sure Mercy that God gave to David. Jeremiah proclaimed it forever. We have the opportunity to participate in that.

In Jeremiah 33:20-22 the Bible says concerning the covenant God made with David:

> *Thus says the LORD: "If you can break My covenant with the day and My covenant with the night, so that there will not be day and night in their season, then My covenant may also be broken with David My*

servant, so that he shall not have a son to reign on his throne, and with the Levites, the priests, My ministers. As the host of heaven cannot be numbered, nor the sand of the sea measured, so will I multiply the descendants of David My servant and the Levites who minister to Me."

Every morning when we see the sun rise and every evening when we see the sun set, we know that the covenant God made with David and the words the Holy Spirit put on his lips for prayer in the Psalms before the Ark are not only ours but they were the core and essence of what made the mighty men an undefeatable force in the earth. Covenant was continually proclaimed before the Ark while the army was engaged in battle. God moved in their behalf. You could not be an enemy of David and live.

Only two "covenants of salt" were made forever in scripture. The offering given to Aaron and tithes given to the Levites is the first. The governmental dominion guaranteeing a line of kings for David through "Sure Mercy" was the second. God does not break covenant. It is easier to stop the rotation of the planets than for God to break covenant! Why is the church sitting down when it needs to be standing up and demonstrating the Judge of all the earth? Are we a nation in the midst of judgment because we have not cleansed the temple, purified the local altar, stood on our covenant and demanded God cut off the enemy? Should we not ask God to move His Hand on judges ruling in favor of homosexual marriage or abortion – sin that fills our land with iniquity? The church has an obligation to make a stand and pray that God cut off those who are defiling the land.

Psalm 2 promises we can ask for the nations and they will be given to us but the enemy has a plan and his plan is to fill those nations with iniquity so they have to be judged before the church comes to fullness of Christ and gets their harvest. I believe God wants to expedite our growth in fullness of Christ and there is no better avenue to grow than embracing the path of justice. A heart-cry for justice demands judgment on the enemies, cutting them off and granting mercy to the nation. The fruit of justice is a harvest for the church.

The Bible says that justice has a voice. Psalm 110:1-2 states, *"The LORD said to my Lord, 'Sit at My right hand, Till I make Your enemies Your footstool.' The LORD shall send the rod of Your strength out of Zion. Rule in the midst of Your enemies!"* The interesting part of this progression is the next verse. Verse 3 says, *"Your people shall be volunteers In the day of Your power; In the beauties of holiness, from the womb of the morning, You have the dew of Your youth."* Without an army of volunteers there is a diminished voice. Somebody has to declare the Word of the Lord. Somebody has to take the covenant in their mouth and declare it. Peter had to declare judgment on Ananias and Sapphira. Paul had to declare blindness on the false prophet. Psalm 141:5 says, *"Let the righteous strike me; It shall be a kindness, And let him reprove me; It shall be as excellent oil; Let my head not refuse it. For still my prayer is **against** the deeds of the wicked."* David understood the necessity of praying against and covenantally cutting off the enemy. Where is this understanding in the church today? Where is the Davidic cry against the enemy? God promises to restore the Tabernacle of David which has fallen down. What if the prophetic fulfillment is a church praying as David prayed against the enemy? It is important to pray "*against*" judges who vote for policies that promote and protect sin. It is important to pray "*against*" those who are defiling the land by their unrighteous decrees. David did not have any problem praying "*against*" and because he prayed – God moved! Because he prayed—God cut off Absalom. Because he prayed—God cut off Ahithophel. Because David prayed—God cut off the enemy and the nation was restored. The Apostle Paul prayed against Alexander the coppersmith. When will the church **pray against** and see enemies cut off so we can gain a harvest and see the nation restored!

In Matthew 12 Jesus declared His intention of taking justice to victory. After His death, burial, and resurrection in Matthew 28, with mission accomplished, He declared, *"All authority has been given to Me in heaven and on earth. Go therefore and make disciples of all the nations, baptizing them in the name of the Father and of the Son and of the Holy Spirit, teaching them to observe all things that I have commanded you; and lo, I am with you always, even to the end of the age."* Because the foundation of God's Throne is justice and righteousness, the "all authority" in heaven and earth includes the authority to bring forth the justice and righteousness of heaven. The entire book of Revelation is about justice being manifested in an unrighteous environment. To represent the God who makes war and judges, we first have to order our own life in harmony with biblical standards. Then and only then do we qualify to stand in the fire we inevitably have to call down. Preparing the church to be an end-time army means preparing for war! It does not get any better. Scripture makes clear that at the end of the age the only justice available is that which comes from the Throne-Room spoken, declared, and decreed by God's people because they are willing to order their life accordingly and qualify to be agents of divine justice.

I was on a trip recently and a woman came to me in tears. I had finished teaching on Jesus and Justice and she related the story of how her daughter had been given a date-rape drug called Rohypnol. By the time they figured out what happened it was too late to collect evidence, but they went to the police with the story. On the same day they went to the police with the name of the young man, he was already before a judge over the same violation in the life of another young woman. The judge dismissed the case and let the young man off. It was obvious this man was a serial rapist who had selected and procured his drug of choice and was going to continue doing the same thing. This mother asked, "Is there any justice for my daughter?" I said, "Yes there is, but we are going to have to invoke the Covenant of Sure Mercy and ask God to cut him off. That means we have to be able to stand in the fire we are calling down." We cannot ask for justice on sexual sin if there is sexual sin anywhere in our life. If we are compromised in the area for which we request justice, we can expect His Judicial Hand to fall on our lives as well."

We joined hands and prayed in agreement. I invoked the Covenant of Sure Mercy. I asked God to cut this young man off and save all the future young women that would be his victims. The next day I had to go home and within six weeks I got an email saying this young man died in a violent motorcycle accident, twenty-one days after we prayed. Representing the Judicial Christ is necessary to accomplish Kingdom purposes. Let us move into the place where our Spirit-led prayers move God's Hand!

The God of Justice is rising in the church and the only thing that is keeping us from manifesting the full measure of what He has in mind is that we do not feel prepared and ready to represent Him. That has to change and it can only change by individual personal choices. To order our life according to God's righteous standards, we qualify to fully represent the Judge of all the earth and to war with Him. The glorious church is calling for volunteers. Will we be a part? Jesus is pouring out an anointing for justice. Certainly every one of us should qualify to carry this anointing. Jesus is ready to judge and make war and is looking for volunteers. Make sure you are found ready. There is a great harvest of nations that is promised, but the resistance is dramatic. It is governmental and it goes to the highest offices in the land. Only those who are thoroughly prepared and ready to bring the justice of God can break through the resistance and open the door for the harvest. The choice to participate is ours. Let Jesus the Judge arise in the church!

Not by your own might or power
Or your own will or strategy,
But by the Spirit of the Lord
May justice-prayers become your plea!

Jayne Houghton

Endnotes

[i] Weymouth, Richard Francis. Hampden-Cook, Ernest. Ed. *The New Testament in Modern Speech*, 3rd Ed. Boston, Pilgrim Press. 1911. Print.

[ii] Kittel, Gerhard, Ed. Theological Dictionary of the New Testament, V. 1. Grand Rapids, WM,B. Eerdmans Publishing Co. 1964. 407 p. Print.

[iii] Ham, Edward E. *50 Years on the Battle Front with Christ: A Biography of Mordecai F. Ham*. Old Kentucky Home Revivalist, 1950. 32 p. Print.

[iv] Rushdooney, Rousas John. *The Foundations of Social Order*. Phillipsburg, Presbyterian & Reformed Publishing Company, 1978. 17 p. Print.

[v] Vincent's Word Studies in the New Testament 4 volumes,. 1887, Marvin R. Vincent Logos Bible Software, 2720 p 2002. Charles Scribner's & Sons, 1887-1995. EPrint.

[vi] Received as a Gift of the Spirit, a word of wisdom, (1 Corinthians 12:8a) by Kingdom Ministries; 2013.

About the Author

Al Houghton is a Father in the Faith formed in the fire. He is a proven prophetic voice who tempers his words by the yardstick of Scripture. Approximately forty years of ministry now include over thirty-three years of Word At Work daily Bible studies, six books & a library of CD and MP3 teaching series that form the foundation for leaders on all seven continents.

In 1975, Al moved to California to attend seminary, obtained a Masters in Divinity degree, and there met and married his wife, Jayne. They began a teaching ministry which moved from home Bible studies to facilities like Mott Auditorium in Pasadena, CA, where he pastored for a decade. Al and Jayne have three children, Jonathan, Julie and Michael.

Jayne has a strong teaching gift and Julie a strong prophetic gift, making their input invaluable in collaboration in the Bible studies and books.

The Houghton's primary assignment is elevating the church into their Kingly Priesthood as "agents of justice." Acts 2:36 says, "Therefore let all the house of Israel know assuredly that God has made this Jesus, whom you crucified both Lord (koo-ree-os) and Christ (khris-tos)." Many believers only know the Priestly CHRIST, but do not know the Judicial LORD. As a result, most believers can "turn-the-other-cheek" but few can swing our Biblical, Judicial Sword.

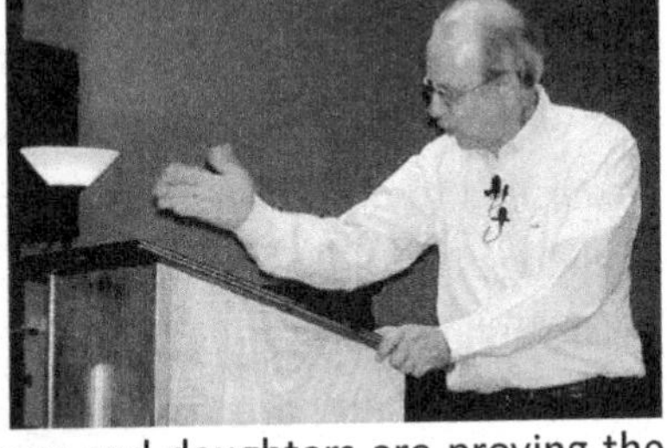

Jesus manifested judicially when Al was first called into ministry. Ten years later, He began participating with the Judicial Christ and through the years has innumerable testimonies of Christ in action from warning to affliction to termination. Al's spiritual sons and daughters are proving the reality of the Judicial Christ among the nations.

GOD'S LAYERED LOVE

Learning to love the way God loves is perhaps the greatest quest we can ever embrace! There are five distinct applications of God's love revealed in Scripture. If we arbitrarily choose to develop in layers we like and avoid those that seem uncomfortable, then we play God. Mature saints seek the Holy Spirit's application. Until we truly accept and pursue love in its entirety, we forfeit God's fullness!

As believers we are called to represent Jesus as both a King and Priest. Those two roles are very different. Raising children requires hugs and handkerchiefs as loving affirmation, but sometimes gives way to afflicting discipline. Training and consequences are essential in character development!

The Apostle Peter was representing Christ when terminating love ended the lives of Ananias and Sapphira. God's love commanded an angel to visit Herod! Love turns the other cheek but also terminates. Are we prepared to participate with the Spirit in termination as Peter was asked to do? God's love is deep and wide. Are we prepared for the challenges of the last days?

The fullness of God's Layered Love guarantees us finishing our race victoriously. Prepare for the greatest harvest ever by growing in the fullness of God's love!

THE SURE MERCIES OF DAVID

How should believers respond to the avalanche of evil assaulting our nation, cursing our biblical culture and outlawing the voices of virtue?

God covenanted with David to redeem his failure and cut off his enemies. David knew what to ask for to save his land, based on this covenant. Jesus guaranteed the covenant of "Sure Mercy" and Paul preached it in Acts 13 with a warning that failure to use it could cost the loss of cities, and even the nation.

"Sure Mercy" empowers the church by putting a two-edged sword in the hand of every believer. The first edge cuts away the guilt, shame and insecurity of personal failure allowing God to transform the failure into a foundation for future prophetic fulfillment. The second edge moves God's Hand to execute biblical justice saving the nation from all those intent on perverting and destroying the land by filling it with iniquity!

Learning the difference between "Sure Mercy" for an individual and "Sure Mercy" for a nation empowers us to pray an entirely different way. David expressed in the Psalms God's heart for victory and His willingness to war in our behalf. This book helps the church war spiritually as David did physically!

MARKED MEN

God has promised end-time protections for His people as we navigate perilous times to accomplish a great end-time harvest. The prophetic tragedy of the last leadership generation is that they primarily equipped the church to recognize the mark of the counterfeit christ. The Bible promises nine real marks from the true Christ, each available for a specific end-time purpose. Almost every believer knows the counterfeit 666, but how many of us can name one of God's nine real marks enabling us to finish our call. Some of the questions answered are:

1. If we gain God's marks, are we protected from premature death till we finish our heavenly assignments? <u>The answer is, yes!</u>
2. Will Jesus come to the church before He comes for it, and if so, for what purpose? <u>Yes, He will. And the purpose will be judgment.</u>
3. If the cup has to be full before we can get a new heavens and earth, doesn't this make the pre-trib, mid and post arguments inconsequential? <u>No, but it does reduce their relevance.</u>
4. Are we preparing our children for the wrong rapture? How should we be training them for the future? <u>Yes – transition!</u>
5. How does the principle of fullness impact the church? Does fullness of iniquity demand fullness of Christ? <u>Bank on it!</u>
6. If in the end people must acquiesce to buy or sell, what must we do to achieve God's promised protection now? <u>Take God's marks.</u>

PURIFYING THE ALTAR

The first consistent manifestations of the Judicial Christ developed as the Lord began unfolding a revelation concerning *Purifying The Altar.* The premier conflict of Scripture rages over our worship. Will we worship God or money? The issue dominated the disciples' relationship for three and one half years. At the last supper, they still could not discern the thief among them because there was "rivalry" over who should be the greatest! Whoever was in charge controlled the purse strings!

Purifying The Altar is a revolutionary and revelatory unfolding of the foundational principles that enable ever believer to stand on a Judicial platform with Christ declaring, decreeing and calling forth His Eternal Will! *Purifying The Altar* opens a whole new paradigm where we cooperate with the Holy Spirit in calling forth His Judicial plan. Isaiah 53:12 reveals that plan contains some radical manifestations, *"Therefore I will divide Him a portion with the great, And He shall divide the spoil with the strong, Because He poured out His soul unto death, And He was numbered with the transgressors, And He bore the sin of many, And made intercession for the transgressors."*

Jesus stated in Matthew 23, *"'Fools and blind! For which is greater, the gift or the altar that sanctifies the gift?'"* Jesus made the condition of the altar the determinant covenant factor. When an altar is cleansed so that it "sanctifies" what is given, the windows of heaven open because the covenant is actually consummated.

> *Purifying The Altar* is a study of the biblical principles which contribute to closing or opening the windows of heaven through purifying both the personal and corporate altars!

CONVERTS OR DISCIPLES?

Converts or Disciples is a prophetic word to the church, hopefully causing a reassessment of our ultimate purpose. If our number one goal is making disciples, then every believer we impact should be empowered to pass the 12 fold test of discipleship reflecting the commitment of the early church as they cultivated an apostolic culture!

1. True discipleship begins when we choose to embrace <u>Lordship</u>.
2. Converts walk where self wants, while disciples walk where <u>God wants.</u>
3. A convert sets his own <u>agenda</u>, while a disciple embraces God's <u>agenda</u>.
4. Converts often reject <u>God's plan</u>, while disciples accept it.
5. Converts use faith to <u>satisfy self</u>, while disciples use it to <u>satisfy God</u>.
6. Converts are oblivious to <u>manipulation</u> while disciples discern it.
7. Disciples volunteer for <u>hazardous duty</u>, while converts hesitate.
8. Disciples dare not covenant with <u>death</u> but converts do it repeatedly.
9. Disciples are vigilant about who their actions <u>worship</u>, but converts are not.
10. Disciples escape financial manipulation because they give by <u>revealed</u> need, while converts usually respond to <u>apparent</u> need.
11. Disciples display <u>Kingly Judicial Authority</u>, while converts do not.
12. Disciples have to extend <u>mercy</u>, while converts think it is optional.

CPSIA information can be obtained
at www.ICGtesting.com
Printed in the USA
FSOW03n1250130915
10961FS

9 780940 252080